D. Bag.

ARRIVAL PRESS

THE POET'S COMPANION

Edited

By

TIM SHARP

First published in Great Britain in 1997 by
ARRIVAL PRESS
1 - 2 Wainman Road, Woodston,
Peterborough, PE2 7BU

HB ISBN 1 85786 474 3
SB ISBN 1 85786 469 7

Foreword

The poets that I have included in this anthology come from all walks of life; housewives and lawyers sit alongside children and senior citizens. Whether you enjoy reading romantic poetry or verse that is humorous or sad, or just any poetic theme, this is the book you will enjoy reading again and again.

I do hope that you enjoy reading this book as much as I did whilst editing it.

Tim Sharp
Editor

CONTENTS

1418

What was that? An eerie cry
of death, that has just passed me by.
How lonely here all by myself
I must keep talking - or else.
Hello there, Jack my bosom pal
How are you now, how's that fine young gal
of yours that you always talk about?
Speak up then man, don't stare like that.
No wait, don't call out just yet
There's someone out there that we've not met.

Hey Jack, wake up the coast is clear
They've passed this way, they came so near
But it's safe now to talk again
Wake up old man - what's that stain
so bright and dark and spreading out
across your chest so fine and stout?
Oh Jack, not you, my friend, my ally
Don't die now Jack, don't die, don't die.

Can someone hear me, can someone see?
I'm all alone here - not you, just me.
It's cold and wet, my body aches
I'm sorry, Mam, for my dirty face.
Can I go home now, I've done my bit
I've held this ground and now I sit
and wait for glory to surround me
but all I find is filth and bloody
monsters with broken limbs and staring eyes -
no breath or speech they cannot lie.
Please God come and take me, I'm so afraid
Don't leave me here, alone, for another day.

Coleen Hickey

1

BALKAN BLUES

Many happy days I spent in sunny Split
And some more in Kranska Gora
What has happened to Yugoslavia
Fills me with complete horror
One day I hope I can return
To visit beautiful Sarajevo
Home of the Winter Olympics '84
I hope soon I will be able
The River Sava tells some tales
From its source near the Austrian border
It runs all the way to Belgrade
Through scenes of abject horror
Slovenians, Croats, Bosnians, Serbs
Are all very proud people
Let's hope all differences can be resolved
We can view peace from the church's onion steeple
The European Community has many faults
but for fifty years, no war
Has taken place between member states
A goal worth working for
In years to come we can but hope
That Europe will be as one
With a joining of all Nations
And the days of conflict done

Alister Lang

AWAKENING FROM THE NIGHTMARE

Life's nothing but a dream
And is never quite what it seems
As it flows like a mountain stream
And as time goes by like the shifting sand
Undisturbed in this deserted land
Never to be touched by human hand

But as it turns
From dream to nightmare
We're awakened by a midnight scare
To leave us in the frightening glare
Of one man's fight for another man's oil
That's lost beneath the frightened soil
But soon to be a foreigner's spoil

And as it gets out of control
We'll just have to play our role
To send this mad man back to his hole
Our damning lesson we'll have to teach
And fight him on this sealess beach

David White

PATIENT NUMBER TWELVE SUBSTITUTE CASE

On visiting days I look into brooding
eyes and see instability.
The tic in your face twitches nervously
around jaws that have to be supported
by shaking hands.
Dark unperceptive eyes blink rapidly
It is obvious you are on the verge
of hysteria, unstable as a badly roped
load on the back of a lorry - but
twice as deadly.
With an ask me no questions I'll
tell you no lies look upon your
face, you sit waiting for substance
to hurtle you back from outer space
Hope one day you'll rejoin the
human race.
But for now you're patient number twelve
Substitute case.

Jean Barr

3

SIX TO SIX-THIRTY

Six pm
The explosion heard
ten kilometres away.
People on balconies, in cars,
aghast at this first of future outrages.

Six-fifteen,
Radios tuned
to island news.
Soft tones announce the day's events
politicians' pronouncements.
The bomb is not admitted.

Six-thirty.
The BBC news
its correspondent at the place of death.
In the bus station, describing.
Bodies splintered among the wreckage
broadcast to the world.
Truth.

Susanne Shalders

SIGN OF THE TIMES

Who's to say a flower, has no soul.
To say we're all out of control.
What say you to a question asked
A volcanic mountain opened at last.
A canned government in a tin of beans.
A world of drugs in its teens.
Cancer unheard of in time.
A decade full of crime.
A year of ozone, a world not heard.
Animal politics! Don't be absurd!

Irra Borthwick

PEACE

Peace . . .
We exert this resounding cry,
Again and again . . .
Asking the question . . . why?
Why do so many needlessly die,
Was peace a deceitful lie?

Fighting wars,
Contempt we feed,
More unrest that we don't need.
Wars caused by demand for power and greed,
Knowing only too well to where it will lead.
Another grievance and another deadly deed.

So many lives lost through war,
Unaware at times . . . not sure what they are fighting for.

Politicians air contempt,
Feelings they vent,
Showing their discontent.
Causing wars that they could/should prevent,
Too far and distant lands
Our troops are sent,
Cannon fodder for the government.

Fighting for peace,
There is just no way . . .
Another case of hypocrisy,
What happened to diplomacy.
There must be another way,
Fighting for peace is irony.
Let the people have a say . . .
Maybe the fighting will delay,
Through discussion we'll make headway.
Peaceful solutions for which we pray.

Stephen McGeeney

CHRISTMAS

Crouching, dodging, sniping boys
Playing with their Christmas toys
Finding guns are fun
Would kill with them if they were men.
Soldier, let me stay alive,
I have this built-in wish to survive.

Josephine Thompson

A PRAYER

Please Jesus, give the people a
sign,
Let them know, you still have them
on your mind,

Let the innocent know that Hope
is not lost,
Give courage and strength to those
who need it most,

Show the people, the truth of the
Script,
Bring them back from wherever they
drift,

Let everyone see, The Light of life
comes from the sun,
Not from shining gold, the profit of
the gun,

Please Jesus, give the people a true
sign,
Clear away the Judas, in everyone's
mind.

J Burge

HIROSHIMA

A blinding flash
The mushroom cloud
Man has a new toy now
This dark knowledge he now employs
Man is now the devil's envoy
Let loose the beast with fiery breath
Man has become death
This is a new pain
Comes the black rain
This dark horror for to tell
Man has found the keys to Hell.

Gerald Williams

A TRUE CHRISTMAS STORY

Our Dad he went out Christmas shopping,
Met some friends kept on stopping,
With everyone he had a drink.
Our Dad just didn't stop to think.
With Christmas fare all in the bag
He started homeward did our Dad
But on the corner of the road
The handle broke and shed its load.
With Christmas goods all scattered round
He found himself upon the ground
Sat there back against the wall
Hadn't felt the bump at all.
Picking it all up, no time for rest
And with the bag clasped to his chest
He hurried on with quickened gait,
Afraid he might arrive home late,
The moral is, so I've been told,
Don't carry more than you can hold!

George Cozens

ANOTHER BLOODY BOMB

Another bloody bomb has dropped
It has exploded in my heart
A life has gone
But mine goes on
It is time to make a fresh start.

Blood has flowed
My blood runs cold
How can one understand
Man's inhumanity to man.

I feel so sad
A bad dose of the blues
I don't want to read the paper
I don't want to hear the news
I don't want to hear about
Another bloody bomb.

I feel lost and helpless
I feel I can't go on
Though I know I must
For throughout the chaos and madness
There is one we can trust
For the pain has brought us to our knees
To pray 'Stop the bloodshed, my God please'
And raise our hearts and gaze above
For through all the madness
We will always have God's love.

Antony Haselton

REPUBLICANISM?

Get rid of the royals,
And to the victor the spoils:
We'll declare ourselves a republic,
And let Scotland and Wales become independent;
We'll even vote for a President,
And return Northern Ireland to its rightful owners;
We'll declare war on separatist movements in Cornwall,
And become a richer and better country because of it

Maybe not.

Paul Talbot

OUR WORLD

What has happened to our world?
Or the people in it, pray,
Everything is changing
In a very frightening way.
Vandals, muggers, drug-pushers too,
Children abused or sniffing glue.
What has happened to us all
I ask myself each day,
Vice and murder all around,
Is there no other way?
Can we not return to peace,
For surely we will pay.
For heaven's sake let's start again,
And learn to deem each one a brother,
And look toward the sun, not rain,
And learn to live beside each other.
Catholic, Protestant, black and white,
No longer feel the need to fight,
And happiness could then abound,
And carefree laughter be the sound.

Rose Coote

I WANT TO BE BRITISH

Why won't the government listen to me,
Because British is what I want to be.
I don't want Europeans saying what we can do,
For what our country needs they haven't a clue.
Our government has enough problems of its own,
And I feel that they should be left alone.
I can see Britain heading for great disaster,
As they rush into things faster and faster.
Many things have been achieved in this country,
And it has had nothing to do with the EEC.

Donna Dibb

TWO SIDES TO THE QUESTION

As they mop their eyes, (I hope they'll be crying)
Will they say 'she tried' - or 'was really trying'?
Will they say 'how well she bore her pain'?
Or 'we won't have to listen to her moaning again.'
Perhaps they'll all say 'her house was so neat'
Or 'so horribly tidy you felt all feet'
They'll remember of course all my sound advice; ← *Though something reminds which wasn't nice*
I'm sure all my witticisms they'll recall;
They certainly weren't criticisms. No not at all.
My classic hair and dress will bring memories outpouring.
'What century does she live in, heavens how boring'
I made interesting conversation, lightened with humour.
'She has ears round each corner, starts every rumour'
At social occasions I really stood out.
All alone in a corner like a pond in a drought.
'She gave in her mite for any good cause.'
'And made sure we all knew it without any pause!'
Oh dear now me and her have met face to face . . .
I'd better start reforming before the end of the race!

Di Bagshawe

10

I VOTED FOR JOHN MAJOR

I know right from wrong, and have always paid my way,
But tell me what's a man to do in Britain here today?
There may not be a pension for those that paid for years,
And pray your God comes quickly, and takes you without tears,
For the State will punish any thrift and any assets seize,
And the bill for care and nursing, will bring you to your knees.
A lifetime spent in work, and a modest nest egg grown,
Will not help your children, they still will want your home.

Meet your maker sooner, better then than late,
Die before you need the care and pay the going rate.
For it's forty percent on exit, the State must have its way
Just one last kick for old time's sake, the dead will have to pay.
They call themselves Conservatives, I don't believe that's true,
They speak like the Conservatives, but see the things they do.

The Englishman left to see his castle, chained and repossessed,
Encouraged to borrow at eight percent, history tells the rest,
Our fishermen and miners, and now our farmers too,
Ruined at the alter of the EEC, but don't dare ask me and you.
And now they cry: 'A billionaire, and a foreigner is here,
He undermines Democracy,' they sound oh so sincere,
But he's as foreign as Mr Portillo, the Minister for our defence,
And since when did Tory coffers, at foreign billionaires, take offence.

This man he knows the price we paid, upon air, and land, and sea,
Knows more than you of Englishfolk, our ways and history,
Thank God for foreign billionaires, we might still yet be free!
Once I voted for John Major, but I never will again,
And I still say I'm a Tory, but I'm never one of them,
A Tory wouldn't tax the dead, nor punish those that tried,
And certainly not give away, our forebear's sacred prize,
To none do we pay homage: 'No Prince of Palma, Deutsche or Spain,'
John Major I should pity you, you think that English is merely a name?

Mark Redgewell

11

THE LIGHT AHEAD

All is not doom and gloom
I promise you,
The world still laughs
Despite its pessimistic view.
Hiroshima, the atom bomb
Killed the land and family life,
Children died hideously, and man
Himself was severed from his wife.
Search our hearts, tell us what to do
To clear the fog from out
Our minds and start anew.

Right then; listen first to nature
And see where we are bent,
Speak out with reason, with knowledge,
Not just passion spent;
Really care what happens,
Not just here in our own patch
But global-wise, put back
The forest fast and set a match
To light the future
That is the right of everyone.
Families, corporates, governments,
Wake up and get this done!

Margaret Baxter

UNTITLED

There was a young lady called Joan
Who was awfully accident prone
Whilst super-glueing a cup
Her friend rang her up
And now Joan can't let go of the 'phone.

Janet Jackson

DEMOCRACY

You can be anything you want to be
Is the meaning of the word democracy
You can say all drugs are bad
While you're having a drink
You can sin, then be forgiven
Without having to think
You can never want to murder
But carry a gun
You can protest against war
Then be glad that we won
You can be a lawyer,
Politician or thief
And still be suppressed
By the power of the police
Fools to believe we are free
With the government laughing at you
Saying 'Yes you are free,
To do as we tell you'
Democracy we can see
Is such a great word
So support it
And let greed and capitalism rule the world

Simon Sinclair

PLENTY OF COMPANY

When I was born I was alone,
I learnt to walk and talk alone,
I started school alone,
When I was sick I was alone,
When I died I was alone,
Now I am buried I have plenty of company!

Julie Allison

WEALTH AND POVERTY

In this decade of the nineties now,
Still brings memories of a lovely time,
We must look beyond the wars and strife,
Changing thoughts and make this world divine,
Lifting spirits, bringing comfort too,
Reaching out a hand, always to another,
Extending to our brothers, all around,
Respecting both our Father and our Mother,
Drugs and aids and drink is rife, but why?
Think about what you really want to be,
Living in the nineties can be fun,
Abusing drugs and solvents, choice is free,
If our youth learns to say the big word, *no*,
For they are people in their own right,
Then the world and life, becomes so good,
There would be less hatred, fears and strife,
Living in the nineties, can be fun,
Raise your thoughts and think what you must do,
Wealth and poverty, you have the right to choose,
The future, our dear youth, belongs to you.

Janette Campbell

LIMERICK

A man on the flying trapeze,
Stopped in need of a sneeze,
He traversed the air,
Missing the chair,
And now speaks
With a very slight wheeze!

Michael John Swain

ADVANCEMENT HAS ITS PRICE

The greatest achievement of the nineties,
And our aim, should be peace,
All attempts to bring this to fruition,
Seem doomed,
One area of the world,
Is pulled back from the brink,
Of self-destruction,
Only to find another outbreak of war,
Elsewhere,

In what we class as the civilised world,
Our own society flounders,
Acts of rape and violence,
Merciless killings,
I fear that good and evil,
Walk side by side,

Greed is man's greatest enemy,
Envy his actions,
Technology advanced in the nineties
Which sadly has its price,
The more knowledge we gain,
The more skilled we become,
We have the finger,
On the button of self-destruct,
Throughout the world,

To have peace, we have to live,
Side by side in harmony,
Prejudice, cast aside,
As the 21st century dawns,
Man needs a miracle,
If this planet, is to survive.

Ann G Wallace

LIFE IN THE 1990'S

What a dreadful world we live in full of greed and lust
I wonder what has happened to decency and trust
Current politicians are largely to blame
Power making policies the name of the game.

Making money is the god of this modern way of life
Cutting costs in public spending causing misery and strife
When will they learn about honesty once more
Bring back humanity is what we implore.

They've had too much power in their hands for far too long
Perhaps the next election will bring a change of song
The men who run the country live in ivory towers
Ignoring all the troubles that are caused by their power.

Listen politicians to what the people say
For if you do not do this you will surely rue the day
Men in high places live lives of luxury
Whilst the workers of this life struggle hard to be free.

From poverty and want which your policies create
Do something *now* before it is too late
The way that we live these days bring grief and despair
So many people and no-one seems to care

When the next election comes and promises are made
Be careful whom you vote for or the price will be paid
Perhaps these little verses will give you food for thought
Think about it e'er you choose avoid being caught.

Verity Denton

THE NINTH DECADE

The nineties we'll remember
How could we all forget
An era that brought changes
It gets harder to accept

We lost our faith in government
Whose good are they working for?
While we're reeling from their latest act
They perform a ncw cncorc

They closed the shipyards and the mines
That made whole townships thrive
Did they ever think, just one of them
How those people would survive?

Violence became the norm
Respect became old-hat
Manners non-existent
Who do we blame for that?

Still out of the ashes a phoenix can rise
Although surprisingly
Who would have thought we'd visit France
On a train beneath the sea

Yes there have been great achievements
Each decade brings its own
But some changes that the nineties brought
Would have been better left alone

Glenda Greeson

MUGGED

I was pushed to the ground,
with a push or a shove.
The next thing I heard was,
Givvus ya bag, luv.
As I turned around, so that I could see,
I was smacked in the mouth,
and, kicked in the knee
I wondered what would happen next,
I felt so helpless and perplexed.
They stole my bag, and both my rings,
The very sentimental things.
To all you muggers around out there,
Get a life.

R D Bowman

CHILDHOOD

If Mary had a little lamb
Why can't I have a gnu?
Of course I know what they are
I've seen them at the zoo.
No. I'll keep it in the garden,
Or maybe the garden shed,
And only let it come indoors
When it is time for bed.

It can sleep in the kitchen,
By the kitchen sink
Then it won't have far to go
If it needs a drink.
Okay then. Let it use the toilet,
We'll get it potty trained.
Oh come on mum. Don't be so cross,
What means scatterbrained?

If I bury these baked beans
In a corner of the lawn,
Will they grow into a beanstalk
Sometime before dawn?
But why are they different
Just because they're in a tin?
Oh come on mum. Please,
I'm not making such a din.

Will you read me a story
When I go to bed?
Or maybe some new nursery rhymes.
They'll do instead.
What's too vivid an imagination?
Have I got as much as dad?
Can I have a drink of water?
Why does my bedtime make you glad?

Letitia M Davies

RAIN FACTORY

Did you know,
Rain grows in Yorkshire.
My mother says that's silly,
'Cos rain doesn't grow.

But by the road,
Near Ferrybridge,
They've got these 'mungous towers,
From which clouds explode.

I think it's silly
To say it doesn't grow.
I've seen it.
So I know.

Jane L Macdonald

THE DENTIST

I woke up with this pain today
I hoped and hoped would go away
The trip I dread I'll have to make
'Cause of that nut stuck in that cake

> The surgery trip not far to go,
> But seems so long, and full of woe.
> With found courage I walk straight in,
> That dreaded drill, a fearful din.

Up I go, my name is called
My heart sinks, I was so bold.
A mask-faced man, tries to calm, to settle,
Gripped in his hands, his sticks of metal.

> Sweat starts to flow, should I run
> The way he talks he finds it fun
> It's a small filling that you require
> If only a stand-in I could hire.

The job is done, I'm over the moon,
Until it's said, that's temporary see you soon.

Nicholas Short

A THORN IN MY SIDE

Hot water, heat, cooking things to eat,
Your functions I can't fault
Your dirt makes me want to bolt
I just can't keep you clean
You simply make me want to scream.

Last night I thought we were on fire
I felt so daft as I opened your draft
I could swear I heard you laugh
The shameful things I said
As I got back into bed.

You're the one thing in this place
That makes things black as the ace of spades
Yet here I am feeding you coal
You dirty great black hungry hole.

Mornings it's your soot I dread
I swear you won't get fed
With all this cleaning my fingers bleed
So dar rayburn take heed
I'm down on one knee, please here my plea
Or you will be the death of me.

Antoinette Spooner

A RAW DEAL

All morning I'd been beating eggs
and folding in the flour.
My future in-laws' visit I expected
on the hour.

At four o'clock the door bell chimed.
Smiles and hugs all around.
How nice to see you both, I said,
come in, please do sit down.

I scurried to the kitchen, my
cakes would win the day,
best china stood most proudly
on the silver tray.

Oven gloves on both my hands
my eyes searched like a sieve.
The empty oven stared back at me . . .
. . . I'd baked them in the fridge!

Vanessa A Hulme

RECIPE FOR DISASTER

To mix and mash, use pot and pans
On hot spots would be potty.
For Mother, when she sees me there
She panics then goes dotty.
For there's one place within my house,
I fear, like a dark hole,
When Mother's temper, on fire, flares up,
Like the chips I charred like charcoal.

I once attempted to produce,
A cake so light and airy,
I prayed when holy tins appeared,
Cake disappeared, scary!

I thought 'At least I can't go wrong,
Heating soup up, even chicken,
Hand bled so bad, cut on the lid,
Ahrgg, where was Stephen King.

Now I've learnt my half baked lesson,
Now rid of, running custard and recipe books.
Just running to switch channel,
From wretched ready, steady, cook.

Jeffrey Crossley

IN TUNE

Nothing will part me from my music,
Or that sweet harmonious cord,
If my life was set to music,
I'd have a tempo and a beat,
My minims and crotchets,
Quietly await their turn,
My semi-breves and quavers,
Would fall into place,
I'd make wonderful music,
To fill that empty space.

Music is like a mother,
Giving life, giving love,
Standing by your side,
Picks you up,
When you are down,
Lifts you even higher,
Offers comfort from the storm,
If music is the food,
Then let's put on a feast,
And let music set the mood.

Each life is an opera,
Composed of highs and lows,
Unfurling its secrets,
With each and every step,
Peace, drama and tranquillity,
All playing their part,
Music is the passion,
Which always rules my heart.

P J Littlefield

KITCHEN CAPERS

I'm in the kitchen to do a curry,
Can't be long, I'm in a hurry.
Boil the rice and chop the meat,
Add rest of stuff, put on the heat.
Chop the onions, eyes a stinging,
Can't see now, oh the 'phone's ringing.
Flip over the safety gate, see who is on the line,
A long chat with an old friend of mine.
Oh no rice boiled dry, my lovely curry, I could cry.
Scrape and scrub the pans, and put them away,
Straight to the chippy for a take away.

Janet Elizabeth Isherwood

LIMERICK

There was a young man from Penzance,
Who longed to indulge in romance,
But the one he would adore had suitors galore
So the poor fellow hadn't a chance.

Reg Morris

TO HELL AND BACK

The capsule starts to slowly recline
The engines begin to grind and whine
Fists are clenched and my body is shaking
The noise drowns out the breaths that I'm taking

Slowly, slowly I open my eyes
Blurred by the lights bright in the sky
Improved by the glasses placed on my face
A vision appears and my heart starts to race

For I'm face to face with a cyclopean giant
Armed with a weapon, his mood seems defiant
A blow in the face leaves me feeling quite numb
A godsend it seems for the torture to come

A masked green man prepares a concoction
Numbers are called like lots at an auction
I whinge and cringe as he drills and scrapes
Then there is calm and I make my escape

At a desk down the hall, I'm handed a bill
My knees give way and my spine starts to chill
For I cracked a tooth on the floor where I fell
And I'm captured again by the dentist from hell!

Joyce Barclay

MOUTHFUL

There ith a young man in Wetht Yorkth,
that hath a bad lithp when he talkth,
He often goeth fithing, and alwayth
keepth withing,
He could thpeak, jutht ath well as
hith thoughth.

K R Griffiths

THE TURKEY WITH TWO LEFT LEGS

On Christmas Eve many years ago,
No turkey had yet been bought
So Mother and I went shopping
Our Christmas dinner we sought.

The market was very crowded
Of turkeys there were very few,
Some large, some small, some damaged
She didn't know what to do.

The one she chose was rather strange
The best of a rather bad lot
You see it only had one drumstick
The other had been given the chop.

She brought a separate drumstick
And sewed it on that night
It was a tricky 'operation'
The result was a comical sight.

One leg was pointing east, the other pointing west,
Although it was an hilarious sight
And left us all in 'stitches',
That Christmas meal was never forgotten
                    - certainly one of the best!

B M Colman

THE BIG, BIG WHEEL

Jack liked the appeal
Of the big wheel
But dad had always said 'no,'
Jack was 'too small'
'Likely to fall'
But still he wanted a go.

So clutching his money
He thought it was funny
To sneak away from his dad's side,
He found his mate
In the queue at the gate
And joined him for the big ride.

Jack looked a sight
As he clung on with fright
To one of the scariest rides,
He wished it would stop
Going over the top
To settle his churning insides.

The ginormous wheel
Had lost its appeal
To Jack who was left feeling bad,
Queasy and shaky,
Wobbly and quaky
He went off in search of his dad.

'Where have you been?
You look rather green'
Cried dad holding burgers to eat,
Jack caught their smell
Felt very unwell
And was sick all over his feet.

Celia Hooker

THE WISE GROOM

To a wedding I went today
'I will' I heard the bride say
As the groom turned to go
He shouted out no
As he hurriedly ran away

Brenda Allen

WISHFUL THINKING

If I could write a book
and tell a tale or two
about so many adventures I would like to do
like sailing over rapids in just a plastic mac
riding on the beach on a turtle's back
hunting wild animals looking for snakes in leaves
swinging with the monkeys through high trees
fighting crocodiles in water up to my knees
climbing mountains high
hand gliding in a clear blue sky
then on to a boat to catch big blue whales
sitting round a camp fire telling tall tales
how I slay'd a dragon in just my vest and shorts
ride on a tiger's back when I get to tired to walk
swim deep down in the sea playing with the sharks
holding on to their fins that would be a lark
riding on an elephant's back through the barren waste
running through the long grass with lions giving chase
riding on a rhino's back
doing a hundred miles an hour on a speedway track
all these I have while I am in my bed,
adventures of a lifetime
are all here in my head.

Winifred Wardle

THE MAN FROM MARS

A man from mars once said,
'I wonder if earthlings are red'
So he hopped in his ship
Down to earth he did nip
But he landed on venus instead

Jacqueline Griffiths

THE ANSWER

So many folk just waste their lives.
Moaning about their bodies.
To counteract this wasteful act.
Just get yourself a hobby.

It doesn't matter what you choose
It's wasteful to sit and weep
Remember it's personality that counts
Beauty is only skin deep.

No cream or lotion gives the glow.
You get from a gentle jog.
And for those with loads of energy.
Get yourself a dog.

Because no amount of cream can erase.
Worry lines from your face.
So make the most of what you've got.
Self pity is such a waste.

Then when you look into the mirror,
Your face looks just the same,
But you will feel so good inside.
You might even feel quite vain.

Jean Monteith

UNTITLED

There once was a boy called Murray,
Who was always cooking hot curry,
The smell was too strong,
Something somewhere was wrong,
Now he's trying his hand at pot pourri!

Fiona H Wilkes

FROM THE EDGE OF THE WORLD

From the edge of the world,
Where we all fall down.
From the point of existence,
Where we make no sound.
When we're spinning and gliding
We turn and we slide into our emptiness . . .

From the depths of a story,
Lost between the lines.
From the haze of our emotion,
Where we guard our lives.
All the feelings and reasons
That struggle to obscure our realities . . .

And the heart of the sunrise,
That dries our eyes.
From floating through shadows,
All the fears and lies.
That spins us and guide us
And turn us and slide us into emptiness . . .

We find a new dawning that sets us down gently,
And pushes us out - from the edge of the world.

Robert Folland

A YOUNG SWIMMER FROM DERRY

There was a young swimmer from Derry,
Who fell from a cross-channel ferry.
He floated for fun
On his back, in the sun
And now he's as brown as a berry.

Veronica Potter

DAD

My dearest Dad you never knew
How much you meant to me.
You were my friend for many years,
Till death took you from me.

I still remember all the times,
We spent just making things.
The little dollies deckchair,
The kite and other things.

All the times we sat together.
Sorting those cigarette cards.
Into sets we perfectly put them.
Making a list called 'special card'.

Then as I grew into maturity.
My son claimed a place in your heart,
You both made tin boats and sorted out 'cards'.
Dear Dad, you are still in my heart.

I look at the flowers my dearest Dad,
And see your face smiling at me.
Remember those gladioli Dad.
It's a secret for you and me.

Jill Pettitt

UNTITLED

There is an editor called Tim
Who must be tall and slim
To arrive in a press
And not look in a mess
With print all over him

Muriel R Wrigley

MTB'ING, IS LIVING

To view the summit
Through sweat soaked eyes,
Aching lungs, exploding thighs,
Reaching the top, goal achieved,
Splendour, beauty, barely believed.

Speed increasing, hurtling downwards,
Tees a blur, friends a flash,
Faster, faster, careful, don't crash,
Apprehension, fear and pleasure,
These mixed feelings, we must endure.

Slowing down, we're on the flat,
Pressing on, across the valley floor,
Rivers, woods, green fields, we adore,
Some day soon, we'll return for more.

Sitting, recovering, now alone,
Memories, thoughts, of the day now gone,
Tomorrow, next week, I must return,
As the countryside, my heart does yearn.

S Baxter

DAVE

A tight, mean old miser called Dave,
Worked all his life just to save,
He boasted to friends
That his life in the end,
Would be spent in a solid gold grave.

Amanda Bayes

UNCERTAIN FUTURE

As the sun sets on another day,
Once again Father Time has had his way.

All the days they seem to fly by,
Floating along like clouds in the sky.

I remember when I was told,
Your best days are before you're old.

With an uncertain future ahead of me,
Maybe my best days are yet to be.

I live each day as it comes to pass,
Life's not for scrutinising with a looking glass.

Life insurance and pension schemes,
Can't see the future in these.

I want to spend my money now,
Don't want no-one to tell me why, when and how.

All my dreams seem to get closer to my touch,
Now my path is set in life no more fighting with myself.

I don't care no more if Father Time is ahead of me,
Whatever comes in life I'm prepared to let it be.

Bob Worm

SWEET STEPHANIE

Sweet Stephanie Hambledon-Tift
Has such an amazing gift,
When at Land's End,
She makes her hair stand on end,
Which gives her a wonderful lift.

Catherine Craft

DEAREST MOTHER

To my dearest Mother, you are No. 1,
If it wasn't for you, my life wouldn't have begun.
How can I forget the yester years,
You brought me up with love and care.
I'm not little anymore as you can see,
Even when I'm old, I still want you next to me.
Remember the cake and candles on my 1st birthday?
I couldn't blow them out, but you showed me the way.
Do you remember when you taught me to walk?
'Mama' I said when I learnt to talk.
You used to wake me in the morning and see me off to school,
I used to make excuses just to skip a lesson or two.
How can I forget when I used to be so weak,
You'd carry me in your arms till I fell asleep.
What did I do to deserve a Mother like you?
It was written in my destiny, it's too good to be true.
Do you remember Dad always telling me off?
I'd come crying to you, in your safe arms I would stop.
The moments we have shared are full of laughter and tears,
We've stuck by each other and we'll do so in the coming years.
There are so many things, but I'm speechless to say,
I'm blessed by a Mother who was destined to come my way.
From the day I was born until the day I die,
I'll always be in debt to you, dearest Mother of mine.

Ashie Rana

FLYING PIG

An adventurous piglet called Troy,
Was reluctant to stay in the sty.
He made his escape
Wearing Superman's cape,
And proved that pigs really can fly!

V Haynes

DEAR DAD

When I think back to my childhood
Happy days were always there
Day trips, holidays, lots of fun
Laughter filled the air
Remember all those cosy nights -
When we sat around the fire?
Singing songs, telling jokes
To our heart's desire!
I was your little blue eyed girl
Always sitting on your knee
Whatever things I longed for
You always bought for me
So just a special thank you Dad,
For all your love and care
I know someday we will meet again
Alas, I know not where!
But I know that you are with me
In everything I do
Bless you Dad, for evermore
There was no-one quite like you!

Esther Godon

COLOMBO

There was a young lady from Colombo,
Who was really a bit of a Bimbo,
She lay on her back,
And let her legs go all slack,
Her legs and her arms were Akimbo.

R Paterson-Howe

HAPPENINGS IN THE FUTURE

I sometimes sit and wonder
What my future holds for me
I often ask myself
A number of questions
Will I ever marry
Have children
Have a nice house
A big house maybe
Will I have a dream car
That controls itself
No tests to pass
Maybe there will be robots
Instead of policemen
That control the world
I don't know what will happen
In the future
But I do know that
I've got a good imagination!

Mellissa Adamson

THERE WAS A YOUNG WOMAN FROM KNUTTON

There was a young woman from Knutton
Who fed her poor husband on mutton,
But one day he turned blue
While eating her stew,
Then he coughed up his wife's missing button.

Peter James O'Rourke

WHAT A LIFE

A Dad relaxed in a chair one day,
'Get a life' his son did say.
Dad looked at him, then heaved a sigh,
In cool, calm, voice, came this reply.
'I had my ups, and took the downs,
Talked with wise men, laughed with clowns.
Walked red carpets, crawled the spoor,
Been robbed by rich, and fed by poor.
Never mugged, or never stole,
Dug up roads, and signed for dole.
Crossed the desert's burning sand,
Chased the foe, with gun in hand,
Sometime struggled, sometime cruised,
Glad the gun was never used.
Loved, and been loved, laughed and cried,
Stood, alone, and could have died.
Life can be cruel, and also special,
So take note son it's no rehearsal.
'Get a life Dad', did you state?
Wish I could at sixty eight!

John Reid

UNTITLED

There was a young man from Wales,
Had a boat with lots of sails,
The wind blew him about,
Which made him shout,
And he was glad to get back to Wales.

E C Williams

POOR OLD DENNIS

Here lies the body
of Dennis Qualxaphthame,
not surprisingly famous
for his unpronounceable name.

Christening him Dennis,
was never that bad
but his unpronounceable surname
drove millions mad!

When applying for work
it was always the same,
who wants a worker
with an unpronounceable name?

This is why poor Dennis
never acquired much wealth -
in fact he couldn't even
pronounce it himself!

So if you're having trouble
reading this epitaph alone -
spare a thought for the engraver
who had to carve his stone!

P J Houghton

LIMERICK

There was a young lady from Devon,
who dreamt she had gone up to heaven.
A voice from the blue
said ' It's too soon for you,
Go back down 'til I call *legs eleven!*

Joan Zambelli

GONE TO A BETTER PLACE

Here lies a woman who liked to spend,
She left not a penny in the end,
Because she knew that life was short
Her bank statement clearly said balance so far nought.

She wasn't slim but wanted to be
A nice size eight and feel comfy,
But in a size twelve she could only just squeeze
If only she didn't like chocolate and cheese.

She tried to skip down life's troubled road,
But sometimes she couldn't carry the load,
But most of the time she spent enjoying herself,
Though she didn't like cooking or dusting the shelf.

She tried to be a helpful girl,
She really wanted to save the world,
Sometimes not tactful, a little bit brash,
Always burnt water and made lumpy mash.

Looked after children though her patience grew thin,
Most of her poems went in the bin,
Incredibly nosy, knew what was going on and where,
So now she's gone to Heaven to see what's going on there.

Tracy Benjafield

VEGGY BURGHERS

Vegetarians living in Brest,
Say: 'Carrots, for eyesight, are best.
    An apple a day
    Keeps the doctor away,
And garlic takes care of the rest.'

Jack Owens

PENNY

Hello Mom, this comes through Pam
Who's able to tell you better than I can

That furry body I recently left
Was only *borrowed* don't feel bereft.

I have not left you, I'm always there,
I'm that gentle whisper, *breathed* on the air

I'm that flash of white tail, that quick blink of eye
You cannot see me as I flit by,

But here I am, you're not alone
I'll never leave my special home

Close your eyes, open your mind
Quietly think and see what you find!

Run with me, have fun with me
I'm young, I'm *new*

I'm back to the kitten the *unknown* gave birth to.
You see, you see, the memories are many.

I'll love you always
From your special *Penny*

Pam Bowyer

UNTITLED

While walking my dog one day,
I heard an old woman say,
'Oh my! Aren't you pert,
And look so alert,
Does your owner always obey?'

Sandra Gibbs

OH JUDGE!

Oh, Judge can't you see
That my dog is the best
He's head and shoulders
Above the rest.

The way that he stands
So proud, so bold.
You can't choose that bitch,
Can't you see that she's old

Last year she got the 'best in show'
Although overweight, and walking too slow
My dog is lively, bright and trim
Next to her he looks quite slim.

She puffs and pants
Around the hall,
Now look at *my* dog
He's on the ball

The cup, it's plain to my dog is due
Listen to the applause I beg of you.
I know the bitch belongs to your sister
But surely you can't let her win again mister?

Maureen Aldous

ROVER'S RETURN

I once had a big spotted dog
Who couldn't be lost in a fog,
Every spot had radar
So he never went far,
Which left all my neighbours agog.

Elizabeth Martin

CASUALTY

Bus stop people
Stared in sadness
At a dead cat
On the road

Gingerly juggernauts
Swung round
Cars slowed down
Seventy sixes crept past
Our thirty-nine went over
Without touching him

Such a clean cat
And fat
Snow crested chest
Three white paws

Boarding the bus
One last look

That's my cat

Ann Sempers

NICOLA

I know a young lady called Nicola,
And by golly I would love to tickle her
But if she declined
When she had been wined and dined
Then I guess I would just have to pickle her.

Peter J Sutton

TAKE CARE OF OUR PLANET

We are only here as caretakers
To look after planet earth,
In our short life span we should do all that we can
Not to destroy our place of birth.
Landscapes disappear by the mile
Cliffs are reclaimed by the ocean,
Crumbling with the weight of the water
And its increasingly destructive motion.
Forests are felled at an alarming rate
New trees must replace those chopped down,
Arable land must be kept for crops
Plants and seeds should be sown.
Earth is becoming so crowded and ravaged
Something must be done,
To stop the destruction before it's too late
And earthly existence is gone.
We try to take good care of ourselves
Why not take care of our planet?
It cannot be too much to ask
That we stop the destruction, can it?

Patricia Frampton

SUPER SUE

A lovely old woman named Sue
decided to use superglue,
but she wouldn't be told
just how quick it takes hold -
now her fingers are stuck to her shoes!

Pamela Murray

DEER

On the hill tops
And in the forests
In the lush green glens
At the water's edge when evening falls
Disguising themselves amid the heather and bracken

Hidden are the fawns
The doe runs amok following her stag
Jumping hedges and fences in pursuit

In the autumn the stags bellow and fight
Twisting their antlers together with all their might
For leadership is their game
And the winner leads his harem 'til spring

On the lowland farm they are bred in their hundreds
And the once rarely seen deer
Can now be seen by all

While man is the hunter
The deer are culled and shot for game
And the once proud and mighty stag fall
For man's foolish gain

Margaret Monaghan

LIMERICK

There once was a worm called Sid,
Who was nervous and always hid,
Coaxed his friends one day,
'Come on out Sid and play,'
When he did he got squashed by a kid!

Tracey Thomson

THE GREY SQUIRREL

A grey squirrel sat
In an old oak tree
Feeling very happy
Seeing acorns there for tea.

His bushy tail was waiving
In the gentle breeze
Saying a big 'thank you'
To all the nutty trees.

Two tiny claws
Were peeling nuts with glee
Filling up his tummy
Which grew tubby as could be.

A pair of bright eyes sparkled
Beholding the lovely sight
A larder in the greenwood
Growing his favourite food delight.

When the grey squirrel
Had eaten up his fill
He collected more for winter
To store inside an old mole hill.

C Porritt

SMARTIE

There once was a little okapi,
Whose mother christened him Smartie;
Should've had stripes on his bottom,
But he just hadn't got 'em,
A spotted okapi was Smartie.

Edna J King

CRUISE MISSILES

I wonder if those 'back room boys'
On far-off distant spheres,
Are blessed or cursed with sayings,
Such as 'All's well my dear' -
Do they take us seriously?
For old planet Earth must seem,
Just a tiny speck in space
Whither a myriad lights do gleam.
Inquiring minds might well ask,
'How far eternity?' Or so . . .
And then rebuffed by the 'old wives' tale',
Like 'One must never know!'
I wonder if science can lend
An ear, to those with set ideas;
Ideas like, 'God is in Our Universe'
Or, 'We rule OK, don't fear!'
And should this planet go off its path
As a shooting star goes thither,
Perhaps some Boffin in the cosmic dust
Will record when we pulled the trigger.

Terrence St John

UNTITLED

A young man who went to Paris
Said 'This is the city for me.
I'll paint on the ponts
I'll climb all the monts,
It's the very best life, you'll agree.

Joyce M Turner

WORLD WAR II

I hate this country
I hate this world
I think this war is just absurd.

I'm angry and confused
as I say 'bye' to Mum
I don't think this journey will be much fun

The terror builds up
as I get on the train
After this war will my life
be the same?

As I sit on my seat
countryside passes by and
I sit there and wonder
will my Mum and Dad die?

Then we get off the train
and are put into a hall
I hope that my name will soon be called

I start getting lonely
and then without being warned
I'm put in a house
and feel very forlorn.

Catherine Whitehouse (10)

THE PROTEST

A Council, when building a road,
Found their plans had been blocked by a toad.
    They thought it no joke
    When he started to croak,
For his protest was made in Morse code.

Margaret Leith Shaw

SARAJEVO

As autumn comes again and coloured leaves
Descend in summer's wake,
The powdered snow clads Sarajevo ridge,
A scene unfolds and now a bridge
Resounds to horse and carriage
And pistol shots ignite the terrors of the 1914 war.
I see a uniform on which a patch of red has spread.
The Archduke Ferdinand and his wife are dead!
And cursed alliances precipitate a global conflict.

Now in the ancient town today
Again death reaches out its hand.
Shades of Belsen lingering yet
Again such vile camps beget.
The host of innocents are moved as in a game
To lose their homes in Ethnic Cleansing's name.
UNO attempts by plane and land to seek its goal
By peaceful means, but these perchance fresh targets make
And trigger-happy fingers take their toll.
Peace-keeping force with helmets blue -
Will Serbs abuse such men as you?

The old man rose at break of day
Some sustenance to find and hunger stay.
A shot . . . he fell upon his face
And clutched two loaves, in death's embrace.

G N Nuttall

47

SPELLBOUND

There once was a fat witch called Ena,
Who was desperate to be a bit leaner,
But while casting the spell,
In her cauldron she fell
And came out, just as fat but much cleaner.

Kay Spurr

D-DAY

The D-Day landings of forty four
Brought home to us all the sorrow of war
Never to be forgotten in our memory
The sacrifices made for you and me
Their courage and bravery will never be known
So many young men so lost and alone
Straight into battle as they waded ashore
The strong the meek the rich and the poor
All had one aim to get the job done
To fight to the end when the battle was won
Thousands of lives were lost that day
On a Normandy Beach so far away
As we look back over fifty years
With a lump in our throat and eyes full of tears
We must remember with the greatest pride
That our boys fought together side by side
It must never be forgotten by each generation
The love in our hearts and pride in our nation.

Joyce Carey

DAISY JONESES

Daisy Joneses vocal tones,
Were completely out of this world,
She could reach a pitch,
That would send a twitch,
Through your body and leave it twirled.

Richard Bright

MAY DAY

Many years ago today
I was crowned, Queen of the May
A wonderful experience that was for me
As all went down on bended knee
We danced we sang with hearts so light
The girls so pretty dressed in white
With crowns of flowers on their heads
Of yellow, blue and different reds
The boys felt very proud to be
Carrying garlands for all to see
The scent from all the different flowers
Seemed to last for hours and hours
It was such a pretty scene
Dancing on the village green
The collecting boxes went around
Some gave a shilling and some a pound
Knowing it was to provide a treat
Later in the summer heat
Sometimes it was a picnic
Sometimes by the sea
No-one worried where it was
They knew that it was free.

J E Bishop

ON THE BOARDS?

A pretty young lady took part -
In a play full of drama to start
Her career on the boards -
And struck quite a chord,
Yet bared nought at all for her art!

Doreen Wheeldon

HERO

I look at you and what do I see?
A man with heart, pride and dignity.
Why did your people treat you so bad?
Maybe you had something, they wish they had.

You crossed bridges that shouldn't be crossed
You won many battles, but you also lost.
You pictured a world, that few can see
You stood tall, and showed what should be.

Why did they judge you? That wasn't right.
All that you did, was carry the fight!
People who loved you, began to lose faith
They seemed to discard you, without a trace.

A fight for freedom is what you led
It wasn't a case of bullets in your head.
With such character and with such strength
You went the distance whatever the length.

Now a different battle you have to face,
In outer limits, the outer space.
But you will win it, you are so strong
Then all the people will know they were wrong.

Gareth Jones

ONE SHOE

There was a man from Peru
who only wore one shoe
and when asked why
he said with a sigh
'They last longer the other's still new.

Dorothy Johnstone

VICTORIA LOMAX

A radiant voice genteel and charming
Fills the air -
Time stood still we were transported
to opera scenes so fair.
A grandchild's gift, her love of song
Did steel away our minds,
the materialistic things of life
were lost awhile.
Our hearts and thoughts
were twined around
one feminine enchanting voice.
Until our hearts and souls were touched,
our eyes grey dim and moist.
Only human voices pure
refresh, rejoice the mind,
bringing back fond memories
that generations bind.
Tall, blonde and very talented is she,
but, 'twas the magic in her voice
that set our spirits free.

Jean Devoy

UNTITLED

There once was a girl called Nelly
Who courted a boy named Kelly
Her friends thought him swell
And wished her well
Then whispered his nickname was Smelly.

B Gibbs

MICKY FINN

He always held his head high with pride
And moved along with a bounce in his stride
With spirits so high he was hard to contain:
And I used to moan when he tugged on the rein
He pulled and he pulled, 'til my fingers were sore
I'd put up with it gladly, just to ride him once more
With big floppy ears and eyes soft and kind
His face will forever be here in my mind.

I learnt a great deal from my four legged friend
And was glad to be there with him, right at the end
His head lay in my arms, as he breathed his last
I could hardly believe his time had passed
He died on the beach, his favourite place.
Where often with Halky and Rags he'd race
And now that he's gone a new life will begin
But I'll never forget my friend Micky Finn.

Lyn Manderson

UNTITLED

A young sailor on deck took a potion,
As he felt very ill from the motion,
But as the waves bounced,
He took more than an ounce,
And exploded all over the ocean.

Eileen M Bailey

MY DAD, YOUR DAD

Dad is big, dad is strong
Dad is just where you come from
Kind in thought, kind in deed
Along with mum, that's all you need
When you are little, reaching up
Holding still your begging cup
Not for food alone . . . 'oh no!'
But help in growing, which way to go.

Then dad is old, his eyes are dim
And you must be right there for him
When he is sad - has work no more
Steer him from that oven door
Talk him through this difficult time
Show him that you do not mind
That he is old and past his best
Only he can put you to the test.

Yvonne S Wirtz

THERE WAS A YOUNG MAN CALLED EDD

There was a young man called Edd
Who once on a hot day said,
'Watch out for the flies,
And don't eat mince pies!
Because if you do you'll get spots on your head!'

Sarah Armstrong

THE THRILL OF THE CHASE

We wait the call, the horn sounds long, we turn and all give chase.
Feel your heart a-pounding as we start to force the pace.
Feel the thrill of speed and skill as each strives for best place.
Feel and taste the challenge as on and on we race.

Who will be the winner, whose the greater deed?
Will the race be won by cunning, by stamina or speed?
Now we're gaining, now we're losing, now we're forging off ahead
And we're giving of our utmost as we follow where he's led.

My legs are getting tired and my hands are stiff and sore,
My back aches with the effort, but we're catching up once more.
We're battered by the wind and rain, we're wet right to the skin,
But we never mind discomfort when the chase it does begin.

Now we're gaining, ever closer, but there's so little time:
Can we hope to catch our quarry before he cross the line?
The horn sounds once, and once again, the finish of the race
And we sail into the jetty, beaten into second place.

Ray Ashworth

LIMERICK

There was an old angler called Todd
Who fell in the sea with his rod.
He gave a loud squeal
As he clung to his reel
And pulled in a dirty great cod.

Sandra Balfour

ECHOES

Sat inside the echoes
Of each other's lives.
Without its gentle humming,
Can we each survive?

On frosty lacquered mornings
Silver wings upon the sky.
We make up the circle:
Angels sing within the eye.

Spirits breathe in harmony:
Pools within the psyche.
Tomorrow met yesterday,
We moved to spirit vibe.

Echoes sound within the circle,
Different paths; but still the hum.
Love moves round in circles,
Since that day it all begun.

Martina Peters

HIGH VOLTAGE

There once was an old man of Torbay
Who had a very cheap toupee
      It was made of Bri-nylon
      He lived under a pylon
That static old man of Torbay!

Jane Wheble

WASTE NOT TASTE

I want to be a gastronome, I try my very best
But my attempts at cordon bleu all end up in a mess.
My stir fry's pretty hopeless; all attempts to use a wok
End up very soggy with a taste that's like old socks.
I tried to cook a sponge cake but it wouldn't rise at all,
I tried to cook a Scotch egg, but I didn't have a ball.
Temptingly before me are the pictures in the book
With captions, so deceiving, saying things like 'easy-cook'.
The moment that my apron's on I know that time is near
When all the flavours of the world completely disappear.
The time for all soufflés to sink, and every cake to burn.
Alas, for all my pains, I'm sure I'll never, ever learn
How to fricassee a duck or make a simple sauce.
(Once I even tried an Adult Education course).
It seems the only way that I'll achieve the taste I want
Is by going to the nearest gastronomic restaurant.

Ann Hobbs

COWARDLY ADVICE?

Mad cows and Englishmen go out in the midday sun
Confusion rears its ugly head;
New day has begun

Stop exporting calves to France
For they have banned our beef
Animal right's groups silenced
Now that is a relief!

Mad cows and Englishmen
Will at last re-*veal*
The truth must now be spoken
Nothing should be concealed

Mad cows lowing in the field
Ministers bellowing in the house
Beef no longer a wholesome yield?
Perhaps we should all eat grouse!

Stephen Friede

CARROT CAKE

The fridge door swung open
the little light came into life,
I grasped at Mother's carrot cake,
no need to use a knife.
The clock struck four,
as I sneaked back to my room
I would blame it on a burglar
if they did not find me soon.
I ate the lot, not a crumb in sight
they'd never know of my secret plight.
Morning came, my face was green
not a word was said,
they knew, they had seen.

Wayne Ford

DOMESTIC BLISS

A la carte meals just aren't my thing
My cordon bleu comes straight from a tin
I burn the toast and over cook an egg
When I'm in the kitchen, you'll wait a long time to be fed.

The local chippy often saves my life
If it wasn't there I'd be in real strife
Kitchen disasters is my middle name
When it comes to cooking I'm just not in the game.

Meal times cause me real stress
At dinner parties I certainly don't impress
As I stand in the kitchen I reach for the phone
Haddock and chips to greet my hubby when he gets home.

Naomi Cooke

THE SOUFFLÉ

Eyes wide, I take a look
At the picture in my cookery book,
My mouth waters, with delight
The fluffy soufflé looks so light,
I mix the ingredients really well
How will it turn out, who can tell,
I place it in the oven, hot
My stomach is tied in a knot,
The timer rings, it's ready now
Before the oven I take a bow,
I open the door so very careful
Is it okay? I'm feeling fearful,
There it is standing tall
Oh no it's starting to fall,
My soufflé may not be quite right
But I can try again another night.

Dawn Kerr

MY KITCHEN 'OH BOTHER!'

Christmas comes but once a year,
Bringing with it, festive cheer,
Mince pies I've been asked to make,
All to help with a Christmas bake, but,
Where's the mince-meat, where's the tin,
In my cupboards, I looked in vain.
Where were they? It's packed! Oh bother!
Having packed, in case we move,
Now that's something I could rue,
For our house, is up for sale, now,
You can hear me wail, oh bother!
When I want a dish for cooking,
In the boxes, I am looking,
Is it this one, is it that, oh bother!
No it's the box, right at the back.
Tonight we'll have, chicken casserole,
Now I'm looking, for that as well.
My measuring jug, has disappeared,
Maybe I'll find it sometime next year!
Many dishes I try to cook,
Yet I have to stop and look, for kitchen crockery. Oh bother!
Next I think I'll make a cake, but,
Where's the bowl, to mix and make?
It's packed, so is the cake tin, oh bother!
At least I have my pots and pans,
To cook my vegetable in, and,
Grill my bacon, cook my meat,
To sit on, I still have a seat, but,
The rest is packed, oh bother!

Rosemary Peach

THE PIE

Today I thought I would bake a pie
And this is no word of a lie
The flour flew all the way up the wall
Along the ceiling right into the hall
Oh why does it have to spill all over
When I open the packet and tear off the cover
The next disaster was the lard
Which was a little too hard
As I chopped it up with the knife
It danced about like a maniac in strife
Then up over the side of the bowl it flew
And the more I chased it the longer it grew
Into ugly big smudges along wall and door
Spilling all over onto the floor
Next came the water that gushed out with a slosh
As it rushed from the jug, oh my, oh gosh
I mixed it and slapped it and pushed it around
It stuck to the basin and on the surround
Ready for rolling I thought with a grin
As I flopped it onto the board to begin
It stuck to the board it stuck to the door
You've never seen such a mess before
I lined the tin, put the filling in
Placed it in the oven ready to begin
Baking, while I cleaned up the mess
Proud of myself and the skills I possess
But as I looked around in dismay
I wondered whatever came over me today
Let this be a lesson to me I thought
The next pie I fancy will be shop bought.

Millicent Boal

DUCHESS OF DEBT

Fergie's in debt, with no cash to spare
She feels, at this moment, that life's so unfair
A million, or three, could be what she owes
But the cause of the debt, everyone knows

A lavish apartment, with staff to attend
Trips on Concorde, to visit a friend
Thousands each week, spent on clothing and shoes
Some of these items, should give her some clues

Now, I have a friend, on the Woodbine estate
Who is also a single parent, called Kate
And she's got some tips, some friendly advice:-
When making a sandwich, just butter *one* slice

Buy all your food at the end of the day
When the supermarkets practically give it away
And only put your heating on
When the kids are home, and the washing's done
(Then you can use the radiators
for drying the clothes, and baking the taters!)

Sleep all together, on cold winter nights
With jumpers and scarves, and thick woolly tights
Dilute the gravy, and use smaller plates
Swap the kids' clothes, with some of their mates'

And if Fergie wants to know more of the same
Forget all the financial advisers of fame
Just ask any housewife on an ordinary street:-
How does she manage to make ends meet?

Margaret Sanderson

DISASTERS

The carrots they stay hard
and the onions I forgot.
There's lumps in the custard
and now I've burnt the pot.
The potatoes boiled dry
and the gravy's one big lump.
I dropped the apple pie
and felt a silly chump.
Often when I'm baking
my neighbours they all know
for I'm very good at making
that smoke alarm go!

P M Low

WHOOPS!

When I'd set up my rod to start fishing,
the weather turned terribly wet.
Rain quickly merged to a torrent,
and soon I was soaked to my neck.

Determined; I fished for some hours,
there's no way that I'd get upset.
But I'd no sort of bite in that downpour.
And I packed up and left with regret.

My partner was waiting to greet me,
on our doorstep she smiled as we met.
She said, 'Come take a look at my salmon,
caught in *'Asda'* with trolley for net.'

Michael Robinson

CHAOS IN THE KITCHEN!

The weekend was looming, our kitchen humming!
Everyone assuming, what should be done
The sink, almost overflowing at the brim,
Angry looking pots and dirty pans,
Suddenly, Mother comes in and demands,
'Where are all those willing hands?'

Looking amazed to find the cat,
Enjoying herself in the midst of all that!
Chaos she loves, plenty to nick and lick,
When suddenly there was a loud click!
To avoid a telling off, hurriedly escaping,
Leaping, almost flying, through the door
She dragged a stack of plates to the floor!

The chaos now was mounting, as Grandma was shouting,
'Those were my best china plates!'
All in pieces now, broken and on the floor.
Amongst all this mess and stress,
A pie was cooking in the oven for tea,
For expected visitors at eight, you see!

Then a sudden knock on the door,
Brought silence to the fore!
The invited guests for dinner at eight,
Managed to come early, instead of late!
But oh dear! No dinner ready or in sight,
The pie, had been forgotten, only cinders to be seen,
It meant the supper would be very lean!

In spite of all the chaos before hand,
Mother, greeted her guests cheerfully and said,
'Lucky the chip-shop is around the corner!'
Little they had known, as to what went on!
This brought back a smile to everyone's face,
And made a happy ending to the day, if only
the cat had stayed away!

Eva Rose

SOIXANTE-NEUF

I've reached a rather awkward stage,
I stare at girls and guess their age,
This stuff called sap, it swells and surges,
And gives me quite surprising urges.
I yearn to go to gigs and dances,
I long for passionate romances,
I often find my heartbeat races,
I'm getting spots in funny places,
I used to plod on with my labours,
Now I want that girl from *Neighbours*,
And what is more, if I was bold,
I'd buy those mags with centrefold,
Instead of Spurs and Leeds United,
Madonna gets me all excited,
Some say it's childish effervescence,
Some say it's only adolescence,
I think they're shooting me a line,
For after all - I'm sixty-nine!

Dave E Priest

REMOVAL MEN'S DILEMMA

It's not a widely known, occurrence
That removal men, before they commence
To attempt, to move any item of furniture
Need to empty their bladders, so as not to get a hernia
It must be difficult, If they haven't had a drink
They must sometimes stop, a long time and think
Of waterfalls, flowing streams, and running water
And wonder, what made them take a job as a porter
They should be supplied, with pints of beer
Then not only could they pass water, but be filled with cheer.

Margaret Crouch

PRODUCTS IN LOVE

One day into the kitchen
To the sink I did proceed
A dish or two to wash and rinse
To tidy up the place

The task I'd undertaken
Required the help I knew
Of some important products
From the press beneath the sink

Joe soap was standing all alone
Maggie rinso was his friend
Then their two companions
Fairy liquid and Brillo pad

A relationship between them
Underneath the sink began
Joe and Maggie fell in love
And the others didn't tell

Fairy liquid did all the work
Until the pans it came
Then quickly to her rescue
Brillo pad had come along

Sure very soon my task was done
With the support of these my friends
Who sat again for another while
Contentedly, within the press.

Catherine O'Kane

PUDDING?

Mother was in a hospital bed,
We three lads left all on our own,
'Well, it's up to us,' Father said,
'To do everything now in this home.'

'So, I will do all of the laundry,'
He said, with a bit of a grin,
'You will do housework and sundry,
And your brother can open tins.'

Well, my brother, a clever chappie,
Decided that this was too tame,
'To make proper meals I'll be happy,
For this cooking's an easy game.'

That night we sat at the table,
Eating a pleasant lamb stew,
To hear a strange noise I was able,
Before the pudding was due.

To go into the kitchen we must,
Because we could stand it no more,
But, such a strange sight met us
As we stood at the kitchen door.

A stalactite clung to the ceiling,
Made of rice pudding it was,
My brother said, with some feeling,
'I think my dessert's a lost cause.'

Because of this cone of goo
He had a short career with food,
A pressure cooker just does not do
For making a creamy, rice pud!

Laura Carlisle

UNTITLED

An artist who worked by the banks of the Nile,
Was famed for his very original style,
You should see what he did
To the great pyramid,
It gave the old Sphinx an inscrutable smile.

Alex McLeish

OFF THE BEATEN TRACK

Back Pack, Pack Back,
Wander off the beaten track.
Meet the people see them smile,
Travel the world for many miles.

Have no fear, most are friends,
From desert sands to mountain's ends.
If they are poor, they are sure to share,
All they have without a care.

Seems to me there is only greed,
Amongst the rich who have no need.
See no problem with race relations.
Silly idea dreamt up by nations.

Governments with lemming like folly,
Who deck the guns with boughs of holly.
Pack back. Back pack.
Home to yet more war alack.

Valerie Miles

THE MAN WHO HATED FLYING

A man won a flight for free,
Taking off he made his last plea,
'I'm so afraid,' he cried,
'Flying's safe,' came the reply,
'But it's the crashing that bothers me!'

James F Kirk

THE FUTURE

We all dream dreams of the future
Just like a wonderful picture
But with fumes from the cars causing so
                              much pollution
Motorways and roundabouts taking so much construction
Taking away the beautiful scenery causing wild life destruction
sprays and fertilisers killing off nature's way of life
Everywhere the land is losing its rife
There soon won't be any natural beauty left
Everything, everywhere is going bereft

The future looks gloomy for the youngsters to cope
As there are no jobs, and not much hope
Education is useless if there is no vacancy
In the line of work that they studied and fancy
So the lovely dream we had for the future
Somehow I don't think they will mature.

Nature Lover

MYSTIC MOG

She sits on my ticket each Saturday night,
Of those juggling numbers I've had not a bite.
Black cats are lucky, or that's what they say,
So how come the Lottery's not come my way?

D Timmis

ZEAL

Two golfers at the R and A,
Set out the famous course to play.
At 8th, in Loop, one tried too hard,
Missed ball and all and fell downward.
His partner hastened him to see,
To give some help if such need be.
Alas, he found his friend quite dead,
So stopped and quietly bowed his head.
What could he do, from Club House far?
His friend, right back, he slow did bear.
In Club House many spoke in praise,
For this brave act did them amaze.
Some of them asked 'How did you manage,
'To play the part of human carriage?'
The golfer, modest, made reply:
'There was one thing, I stress that I
'Felt keen as homeward I him brought.
"Twas up and down between each shot!'

Arthur H Kirkby

PROPER MAYONNAISE
(A letter of complaint)

What has become of mayonnaise?
I've looked for it for many days.
But it has vanished far from sight,
And in its place something called 'Light'.
It may be better for the waist,
I cannot say that for the taste!
So please go back to days of yore
And let us all buy Heinz once more.

Patricia Patterson

MY MOTORBIKE HAS NINE LIVES

My motorbike has nine lives
And that's how it survives
Going round a bend
On the wrong side of the road,
My motorbike has nine lives.

My motorbike has nine lives
And anyone who drives
I'll give them a fright
But we'll never crash,
My motorbike has nine lives.

My motorbike has nine lives,
At each place I arrive
They wonder how I am still in one piece
But my motorbike has nine lives.

Malcolm Lisle

SPIDER

A spider is a little bug,
And it climbs up the bathroom plug,
'Hello' is all it wants to say,
But they all cry and run away.
They run out in robes and towels,
With screams and shouts and sometimes howls,
I don't know what the spider ever did,
Or why they're afraid of a tiny arachnid.

A Martin

TERMINUS

As year on year goes rolling by, our terminus draws near,
With age acceptance is at hand, the outcome is quite clear,
On reaching seventy years one finds that thoughts eternal
cease to mind.
The aspirations now are gone, your three score years and
ten are run.

Although the spring is running down, and hair is grey which
once was brown,
If words count now instead of deeds, imagination intercedes.
A dimpled cheek, a shapely thigh, still brings a twinkle to the eye.

The heart finds joy in looking back, down the long sequestered track.
To friends who journeyed with you there, when life was lived
without a care.
Those happy moments you will find are painted brightly on the mind.
The love once shared, the hopes, the pain, those golden memories remain.

All things which flower will mature, an end will follow that is sure.
So as the journey's end draws near, the unknown future holds no fear,
For when the blossom fades away, the seed I know will grow one day!

L Muscroft

WASHING UP

When I have done the washing up
Some clever dick will find a cup
A plate or two, or maybe three
And darned well hand them all to me.

Now that's the time that I rebel
I lose my cool and start to yell
I've cooked your meals you lazy lot
Those dirty crocks can go to pot.

The water's there just at the sink
And you're all fit and in the pink
Just force yourselves and have a go
It might be fun, you never know.

So hubby says he'll cook a meal
But wash the pots? He's a downright heel
I know that I will have to pay
For any food he cooks that day.

And that's the biggest pain of all
How can he cook a meal so small
Yet dirty all those pots and pans
He should have turned out something grand.

But right before my very eyes
He dishes up his big surprise
A slice of toast, some warmed up beans
That's his idea of haute cuisine

Perhaps one day I'll win the pools
And end up breaking all the rules
'Cause I will change and be much posher
And go and buy a big dishwasher.

R Tyllyer

THE OLD SPITTOON

Jake downed a shot of 'redeye' in the Rising Sun saloon
And muttered silent curses as he missed the old spittoon.
He chewed upon his 'backy and he tried another shot
But, as before, he hit the floor and failed to reach the pot.

One night in a poker game some angry words were spoken
Leading to a bar-room brawl. The old spittoon was broken.
'I sure will miss that old spittoon.' Said Jake to Kansas Kid
And Kansas sighed as he replied 'Yeah! You always did!'

Dennis Turner

AFTER-LIFE

Under grey skies I sit sleepy in gloom, dreamy:
Remembering a distant beach, water blue,
Silver sand; stirring strands of self.

Air itself grasped Purity,
expanding vision, enfolding breath and mind.
Being explodes in discovery,
unfound in Northern Climbs.

Huddled in concrete crypts, sense
Is contained by costive canyons, hardening.

Under such shrouds,
I fly again in sense to pen space,
Virgin air, white waters, sand, sunlit days.

Encountering a freer way, fulfilment
Uncluttered by garbaged lives
Seeking salvation Hades Way.

C M O'Connell

KEEP FIT FANATIC

Show me a pair of trainers
And my heart will fill with glee
An energetic life I love
Watching telly is not for me!

I love to run and swim and cycle
At badminton I'm really keen
I'm happiest when I'm sweating
'Cos it helps to keep you lean!

My zest for fitness knows no bounds
I'm out there come what may
Sunshine, wind, rain and snow
'You must be mad' - I've heard people say!

But fellow fanatics will understand
The drive that spurs us to go
It gives you an exhilarating feeling
Matched with a healthy glow!

The downside to all this fitness
Is the injuries they invoke
Torn muscles, sprains and fractures
But your willpower can't be broke!

So although couch potatoes hate us
They all think we're really mad
There's such a lot of fun they're missing
And I think that's really sad!

Carol Ann Jones

MY SPORT - ORIENTEERING

The Thought Sport, they call it - the name of the game
That's captured my heart so completely.
Red-faced, open-mouthed and gasping for breath -
Why does it cajole me so sweetly?

As I go through the week, I relish the thought
Of my fight with the brambles and heather;
The hills and the fences; the ditches and streams;
Oh yes - and of course there's the weather!

But this is the best - and I've left it till last,
'Cos I know it's a hard act to follow,
It's the *Mud* that entices me squishily on,
There's nothing such fun as a *Wallow*!

Chris Strophair

BURNING THE TREES

In the amazon jungle,
Which we meant to save,
Is weekly burnt an area,
As large as the whole of Wales.

This is meant for farming,
Upon a very poor soil,
Which, when the nutrients are used up,
Will fail them, one and all.

The eroded earth goes into rivers,
The rivers are clotted up,
And the top soil is gone for good,
With very little fuss.

So what was thriving jungle,
That could sustain a tribe,
Is an area of wasteland,
Where Indians cannot live.

M J Phelps

THOUGHTS ON TRAVEL

When abroad, there's always flies,
And foreigners may think we're spies.
Language is a drawback too;
(Embarrassing to 'mime' the Loo!)
The food does not suit our palate;
Why don't they serve us 'beef and carrot?'
Next year we think we'll stay at home.
We'll watch the *rain* (and have a moan!)

H M Birch

SETTING A GOAL

Now that I've reached a later stage in life
My days have changed
I was determined things would vary
They wouldn't stay the same
I set myself a goal
To do the things I'd never done
Enjoying the mature years with
An element of fun
I've found a hobby that I love
Writing rhymes and prose
Going for long country walks
Enjoying plays and shows
You see that when you're older
Don't think that it's too late
To still set goals and to achieve
Add purpose to your days.

Jeanette Gaffney

REFLECTIONS ON GOLF

When I stand upon the tee
I always hope to get that birdie
Straight down the middle, that's my aim
Who said golf was an easy game?
Please don't hook and please don't slice
Go where I want and I'll be nice
Don't go in the water or the trees
Boy these golfers are hard to please!
Golf ball please go where I want you to
That way I won't be turning the air blue
On the fairway and all is going well
Unlike my normal weekly round of hell
The life of a golfer can be really tough
Especially when you're always in the rough
The iron comes out, just one good shot
I've lined it up and picked my spot
The swing's in motion and I follow through
Straight in the water right next to you
I pay the penalty and I take a drop
One day this slice of mine will stop
Just a little pitch shot up to the hole
But there is a slope that takes its toll
Just one good putt is all it takes
But I misread it and away it breaks
I've changed my stance and my grip
But still I let those par scores slip
One good hole can keep your hopes alive
One bad hole and your spirits take a dive
Golf is a game full of so much sorrow
I think I'll go again tomorrow!

Paul Lagdon

ARMCHAIR TRAVELLER

Sapphire sea sips silver shore
Here Paradise is what I saw.
Emerald palm trees fringe this land
Beside untrodden diamond sand.
Horizon lit by ruby sun
Highlights jet figures having fun.

Frozen snow so crisp and white
Reflects expressions of delight -
For Santa's near, with toy-stocked loft;
Reindeer with antlers velvet soft.
This place of dreams makes all believe
What they hope for, they will receive.

With life the organ now pulsates:
A Hong Kong street where no-one waits.
Financial markets rise and fall -
For here they know winner takes all.
Rickshaws and bicycles compete
With glamorous cars in the street.

The Eiffel Tower pierces the sky;
Below, the Seine slides slowly by.
Bright bistros border boulevards,
Where street-stalls offer proud postcards.
The Moulin Rouge invites me in
To see the show soon to begin.

The credits rise upon the screen.
I dwell on where I thought I'd been,
But I must turn to what is real,
Control this wanderlust I feel.
I know that I shall not go there,
Other than curled in an armchair.

Nicky Dicken-Fuller

SEASIDE

When I was a child, we went to the sea,
Daddy and Mummy and Tony and me.
I dropped my toy lamb off the end of the pier;
A fisherman saved it . . . Dad bought him a beer.

We stayed in a boarding house down by the quay;
The landlady fussed over Tony and me.
She made us some cakes with pink icing on top,
And offered us beakers of warm ginger pop.

We went for a trip in Dad's richer friend's yacht.
Poor Tony was seasick, but said he was not.
I fancied myself in the Skipper's peaked cap;
Flo, his wife, let me sit in her blue cotton lap.

Mummy and Daddy caught fish for our tea,
But they were too squirmy and slimy for me,
So I didn't look, but just sucked my thumb
And played with a little white puppy called Chum.

He lived on the boat with the Skipper, old Mick,
Who was kind, and mopped-up after Tony was sick.
He let me take the wheel, his hands over mine,
And then he helped Mummy to reel in her line.

It got a bit rough coming home through the Bay,
Mick said he'd take us out again the next day,
But Tony said he'd rather stay on dry land,
So Mum promised she'd take us two on the sand.

The rest of the holiday went in a flash.
Dad said that quite soon he would run out of cash,
So we travelled back home on the Saturday train,
After promising next year we'd come back again.

But then war broke out, and we never did go.
I wonder what happened to Chum, Mick, and Flo?

June Trelawny

THE SPRINT

In position on the track
Waiting for the gun to crack
Judges give the all clear
Now the nerves and the fear.
One last glance across the line
At the starter, things feel fine.
Another look down the lane
See the tape under strain.

The crack from the gun
Pushing hard for the run
Breathing deep and breathing hard
Lungs bursting with every yard.
First through the tape, what a feeling
To hear the crowd all cheering.

T Read

ME AND MY BIKE!

Pin back your lug-holes and let me tell
The canny tale of the Beaumont Belle.
Don't be daft, man, that's my bike,
But you can call *me* that as well if you like.

You must admit we're a bonny sight,
Travelling along at the speed of light.
Folks stop and stare as we go by,
I'm as proud as punch as I catch their eye.

I'd like to give them a royal wave
And maybe bow my head all brave,
But dashing in and out of cars,
I daren't take my hands off the handle bars!

Ellen Beaumont

YOU WHAT?

'Are you coming out to play?'
Asked my brother-in-law one day.
I told him to go away,
No way I'm playing golf!

I've seen them from the motorway
At that ridiculous game they play,
Shouting 'fore!', or whatever they say,
No way I'm playing golf!

I mean, have you seen the strides they wear?
All dressed like clones of Rupert Bear?
And those two-tone brogues? I wouldn't dare!
No way I'm playing golf!

They all wear Country-Squire cheese-cutter hats
And pay a month's wages for a bag full of bats
And they wear a single glove, the prats,
No way I'm playing golf!

They say things like 'borrow from the nap.'
And discuss their medal handicap
And exclaim things like, 'good shot, old chap!'
No way I'm playing golf!

Then there's bogies, and green-fees, and kilties (on shoes),
And match-play, and Stableford points you can lose,
And hooks, fades and slices, and nineteenth hole booze,
No way I'm playing golf!

But there are also those Sundays, when six shots ahead,
On the sunny fifteenth, and I've left him for dead.
'What? Yes, I have read this poem,
Yes, I know what I said.'
'I'm just kidding, I love playing golf!'

Steve Sutton

MAGIC MUSIC

Share with me the magic
The sound of music can bring
That fills your heart with pleasure
And makes you want to sing.

To hear a promenade concert
To most is sheer delight
Listening to strings and timpani
Harmonise with all their might.

Echoing and re-echoing
Fine and grand concertos
Picking you up and letting you down
With their great crescendos.

Then on a gentler note
As sunshine after rain
The orchestra plays softly
And calms you down again.

You can even be lulled to sleep
As if floating on the ocean
And wake up to the cheers
Of the promenader's standing ovation!

There is music for every season
We look forward to the change
Following our traditions
We have a very wide range.

And when we sing Home Sweet Home
And Never More to Roam
We always have our music
To take us to the moon.

Barbara Fosh

SEVENTY FIVE YEARS ON

There's been a revolution, which effects the human race,
The War Lords and criminals, are in a prison out in space.
There is a World Parliament, which is orbiting the Earth,
Where an ever-lasting peace, has finally given birth.

Some Nations keep their Monarchs, if that's what they want to do,
Others keep their Presidents, and their own elections too,
All must be democracies, so their Governments renew,
Elect a World Parliament, is something they have to do.

Tools of war have been destroyed, and relevant data too,
A censor for inventors, ensures they do not renew.
There's a purge on earthly crime, lots more people do behave,
Children learn self-discipline, from the cradle to the grave.

There's a change of attitudes, throughout all the human race,
Drugs, lust, greed and tobacco, have disappeared, without trace.
People share their expertise, with those who are in decline,
There's a willingness to give, much more freely of their time.

There have been new inventions, to clean up polluting cars,
With microwave powered engines, which was given all the stars.
The fuel is only water, with a plentiful supply,
It made most people happy, but made oil producers cry.

Air travel is much faster, than it's ever been before,
It's also that much safer, so that people travel more.
Aeroplanes look like saucers, and are absolutely new,
They have vertical take off, and they are quite noiseless too.

It's looking in the future, that this story's all about.
There's so much I could tell you, but my time has now run out.
There is another message, that has come from outer space,
Don't colonise their planet, to create another race.

Eric H Barley

A NEW DAWN

Computerised efficiency,
A peerless masterpiece . . .
My objective is confirmed now,
It's time to end a lease . . .

For I, (the last prodigious child
Of man's affair with science),
Have made my father's obsolete,
What now is their appliance?

They presumed that two and two
Would always end up four
But I can make it five or ten
Or any other score.

How they cry out for mercy
But I am unable to comply . . .
I cannot access emotion and
Screens just cannot cry . . .

So each program will delete it,
Yes. . . mercy joins the list
Of idle words and concepts that
My function must resist.

While the old regimes come crashing down
A new dawn slowly breaks
And I am its logical master
For I never make misStak;eS?/.

Anthony Hilton

A DREAM FUTURE

It tinkles in my mind like a clear running stream
A yearning, a longing, my precious golden dream
Something good's coming, just you wait and see
But it's not my dream, for that just cannot be!

Mary Hayworth

MOTHER NATURE IS NOT HAPPY

It's time to take care
It's time to take note
It's time to check your actions
Mother Nature's in revolt

Earthquakes and floods
Drought and heavy rain
She's showing her anger
Again and again

Volcanoes explode
Showering rocks and ash
You cannot buy this lady
With any pile of cash

Mother Nature's not happy
She's telling us so
And if we can't listen
We'll be the first to go

R A Quinney

FOR KEN

I'm writing about a special dad,
who means the world to me.
I've watched him with his children,
as he bounced them on his knee.

He has always been so patient,
always kind and fair.
Sorting out all their problems,
always being there!

He's listened to their worries,
soothed them when they cried.
Never too much in a hurry,
never turning aside.

Always there to help them,
if they should trip or fall.
He'd bring a smile on a rainy day.
He's the greatest dad of all.

You might ask why I'm writing
of someone else's dad.
Or why I think that he's the best,
those children could have had.

For I've watched that man prepared them,
for the challenge that is life.
He's taught them everything they know.
How to cope with cares and strife.

He's a father in a million
set in a class above.
How do I know? I married him!
He's my *children's* dad - My love.

Jenny Smith

ODE TO OUR DAD

Who always mended broken trains and straightened buckled track?
Who gave help with homework and made a leapfrog 'back'?
Who went back and forth to Brownies, and later to Girl Guides?
Who carried all the camping gear across wet fields for miles?

Whose face was always smiling? If disappointment was displayed
Who always told the reasons for the judgements he had made?
Who made quite clear to all of us our punishments were just.
We never questioned right or wrong, we held him in such trust.

Our Dad was someone wonderful, someone to respect.
He had a sense of humour and a quiet intellect.
Our Dad taught us many things, and we thank God above
That the best thing our Dad taught us was to give our children love.

A Edney

A WIFE'S EPITAPH

My life was ended with a sigh,
and now within my grave I lie.
No worries now, no work to do,
no running round after you.
No washing, ironing or the rest,
now I can do what I do best.
Sleep and rest, and feel no pain,
till it's time to walk this earth again.
When next I do, if I can,
Then I'll make sure that I'm a man.

J Stephen

UNCLE EDDIE

He was never very lucky
but he never made much fuss.
Though he gambled quite profusely
he never won that much.
But he always made the effort
and he always wore a smile.
And though his clothes seemed
sometimes ragged,
he wore them with some style.

He complained a little sometimes
that he'd left it all too late.
At optimistic moments
he'd put this down to fate.
And he carried on regardless
but he never had much luck.
That fateful summer evening,
he was killed by a blind white duck.

So fellow friends and mourners
as we're gathered here today,
let us join our hands together,
and together let us pray.
A prayer for Uncle Eddie
for he never had much luck.
And a moments though
on his final words . . .
'God damn that blind white duck.'

J N Roberts

THE GARDENER'S LAMENT

We certainly get a lot of it
Is what the gardeners cry
I often wonder what they mean
As the allotments I pass by
Is it rain or is it shine
Is it frost or is it wind
Or is just a frame of mind
Whatever it is they'll have some more
But it's rarely the kind they are hoping for.

H Hayes

IT'S WITNESSED!

In a field not far from here,
A tree stands proud and clear,
It's in a great open space,
It looks out of place,
Its roots can't tangle with other trees,
Or its leaves rustle together in a winter breeze,
It can't participate in that forever struggle for water,
It just sits and waits for slaughter,
That so openly it witnesses there,
He just has to sit there as if he didn't care,
But he does he is alive like you and me,
Even if he can't hear talk or see,
He was created for nature's benefits,
Not somewhere for us to write or sit,
A tree stands proud and clear,
In a field not far from here.

Karen Waite (13)

HOW I WISH!

Poet, musician, dilettante,
His gifts were many, his faults were scanty;
Kind and generous, a loyal friend,
Giving, forgiving to the end;
Unassuming (he knew his place),
Gentle and courteous, full of grace;
He loved most men - most women, too -
A nobler soul you never knew . . .

How I wish people hadn't lied
But had said those things *before* I died!

Aubrey Woolman

REMEMBER ME NOT AUNTIE AGNES

They all stood there around my grave,
I laid there still, but I wanted to wave.
The ones who cried they made me glad,
As most of them to me were bad.
Then over there is Uncle Bert,
He's telling them all he once kissed my hurt.
But where are the nice words, come on only a few,
Oh dear Auntie Agnes, cor that fart did narth poo!
There's Uncle Andy, He's breaking his heart,
And guess what, Auntie Agnes is hiding behind a cart.
I think they will remember a lot of this day,
But not of me only, probably Auntie Agnes' ways!

Karla Hutchins

I FORGOT!

Here is the grave of Jeanie
Her final resting place.
Dear, departed darling
Lived life at such a pace.
Her memory was not so good
She did forget a lot.
Remembering was not for her
Tied hankies in a knot.
Her life cut short so cruelly
The car came like a shot.
'Why didn't you look both ways?'
Her dying words 'I forgot!'

Corinne England

MY PAL

He's just a dog some would say
But he's more to me in every way
He comforts me when I am sad
And does his best to make me feel glad
He always listens to my chat
And of course never answers back
He is my pal and beloved friend
And I will care for him to the end
When the day comes and we have to part
I know that it will break my heart
Yet one day somewhere on high
I know we'll meet again my pal and I.

Mary Powell

CURTAIN CALL

I was shy when the wide world I entered
And spent many years going red
But then I put things into perspective
And thought I'd become bold instead
I would speak out and risk being lippy
Go first and pretend I weren't meek
And changed sombre for bright garish colours
Which would have looked better if sleek!
I took to the boards doing dramatics
Played floozies, not *me* for the char
Did not bat an eyelid or get nervous
When in a play I was the star
It worked wonders for *me* . . . but my mother
Who'd had to protect me when mild
Found it strange when friends said 'what! *your daughter?*
She'd not boo a goose as a child'
I had wonderful years on this planet
Good family, and lots of friends too
Been to so many exotic places
And had chances not all folk do
But I'm pleased that I started off humble
As that's what life is all about
And when I was told that my time was up
I knew it's not manners to shout
I have done all my laughing and living
I'll leave you dah-lings with a smile
It's only the end of Act One loves
I'll see you again in a while.

Yvonne Docwra

DEDICATION

There comes a time when we must give over
No longer walking from London to Dover.
The years have been given each day to others
Helping along our sisters and brothers,
Not thinking of self when there's work to be done
Having no time for laughter or fun.
But our reward will surely be
A good relaxing time for me.

Barbara Dearness

LULLABY FOR A BABY SQUIRREL

Sleep my child and rest your head
Upon your paws of fiery red.
Close your eyes with lashes long,
Wrap your tail around this sleeping song.
Think not of days when preyed upon,
For now at night they are long gone.
I fear they will be back one day,
'Til then you're safe up in your drey.

Hunted down by hearts of stone,
But now you shiver all alone
You remember now their hungry eyes
Their features you learnt to despise.
Then the chase along the ground
Through the trees 'til you couldn't be found,
You hid in your drey and began to scream
You remember this as you begin to dream,
But now your hunters, they have dined
And you can sleep with peace of mind.

Jill Claire Jones

THE SEASONS

Spring comes with a gentle breeze,
Playing with the flowers,
Rustling the leafy trees
Into April showers.
Nesting birds sing every day,
Gentle little lambs at play.

Summer comes with skies of blue
Upwards wings the lark,
Murmurs of the honey bee
Meetings in the park,
Everyday when work is done
Resting in the fading sun.

Autumn comes with misty haze
Ungrateful is the breeze
Tossing fallen leaves ablaze
Underneath the trees.
Meadows full of new mown hay,
Nuts and fruits and bonfires gay.

Winter comes with frosty night
Icicles on the pane,
Now the lights are shining bright
Till springtime comes again.
Everything is chill and cold
Relentless as the year grows old.

Joan Heybourn

THE GOLDEN GATE

I've got some news but it isn't good, I went in and by the window I stood.
It seemed to me, that we can't be free, from that familiar sound from 93.
The Golden Gate, does not want to wait, until we are at least 98.
It's calling us all, not like before when you could at least get, to 84.

It was one or two a year or more, but now we've got to three or four.
The sad thing is, it's calling our kids, and how much more do we
                                                            need to give.
Our duties lie with those left behind, and together, we must all make a stand.
Untied families is what we want, untied together, we will make a point.

At the gate they'll stand and wait, for him to decide upon their fate.
Righteous ones will walk on through, the other ones will have to queue.
'Lord . . . why do we have to suffer now? Why can't we just live like, how.
The way you teach us through your word; the way you showed us by
                                                            your Birth.'

Remember those left behind, whose lives have changed so sudden.
Friends watching with guilt and fear within, and pray that this does not
                                                            happen to them.
To the ones they love and depend on so, that they could not really let them go.
'Lord . . . how could I cope, if I too lost my folks? I really just, could not,
                                                            imagine this.'

The Lord is our Salvation and our Light, and with him we'll put up a fight.
Trust in him always and together, we will win.
The Golden Gate, can call you at any time, to take a spin.
Whether you are young, in the middle or at the end.
You should always be at one, with the Lord, our Friend.
For he is the pathway through the Golden Gate,
and he will never ever, make you or us, wait.

H M Sweeney

CATHEDRAL OF DURHAM

Trees tall - regal sentinels by the Wear's edge
Theirs - guarding duties - their dying pledge
Protecting tombs - Saint Cuthbert's and Saint Bede's
Those men of great reverence and saintly deeds
Cathedral of Durham - Prince Bishop's Holy see
Where Pilgrims paid homage on bended knee
At this cathedral altar - for one thousand years
The pillage and destruction - it braved with many tears
Serenity is your cassock - Lord with thee abide
Staunch Island palace - near to the castle's side

R Jennings-McCormick

DISAPPEARING ACT

Night's beauty here is cool. Unfurled,
summer dark is slow to fall,
this side of the coloured world.
In the southern hemisphere
it comes on tiptoe, quickly - here!
Twilight is a slice of fear.
Within the city's walls by night
the streets are cleaned. But still, unease
creeps everywhere and questions end.
City kids curl up like snails.
Sleep has overcome their fright
and betrays them. Childhood fails
against death trickled in the ear,
curled like shells. No-one was near.
Better not to see or hear
what happens in the night.

Patience Tuckwell

'SAM' THE HANDFUL

Time now for grooming, come along Sam,
You don't want to come, I don't care a damn.
Up on the bench, there's a good boy,
Not on my shoulders, I'm not your play toy.
Oh! Now off the bench and onto the floor,
Watch him now he will head for the door.
Sit on him Andrew . . . hold him quite still,
I think that I will give him a pill.
Or maybe not, he may get a bit worse,
And then you will hear me utter a curse.
I must get those knots out and make you look fine,
And brush up your coat to a wonderful shine.
Sit on him Andrew . . . tread on his toe,
But whatever you do don't let him go.
Hold him quite firm and hold him right down,
Sam do stop acting like a great circus clown.
Now you're quite smart and nearly quite ready,
To get in that ring, so please stand quite steady.
Julie is shattered, and Andrew is cross,
But what can we do Sam is the boss.
You're only a baby and bound to improve,
We have just got to get you into the groove.
You make us so mad, you think it's a game,
But honestly Sam we love you the same.
One day in the future when you take a top win,
I'll stick out my chest and hold up my chin.
And say it was worth all the hassle and strife,
Because you're the best boy for the rest of your life.

Frances Cook

MY ENGLISH SETTER

Immobile
Whipped by wind and rain,
Head up to wind
Just like the vane
On the church tower spire.

Instinctively
With paw held high
A tail held straight
His looks belie
The speed with which he'll move.

Relentlessly
True to his name
He'll course the moor
To set the game
To flush the birds from cover.

Tirelessly
Forever true
While breath remains
He'll work for you
This gentleman by nature.

Accessory
Before the fact
No murderous soul is he
He's gentle, kind, devoted
And will never cease to be
My faithful friend and helper.

Jill Collis

THOUGHTS OF A PEKINGESE

The forbidden city was my domain
I have walked where Emperors reign.
On silken cushions I took my rest
And by Buddha's kiss I was truly blest.

Vivienne Lee

BABY FOX

Baby fox all sad, forlorn,
Has seen his mother's body torn
By hounds that chased her over the hill,
Swiftly closing for the kill.

His fate now he does not know,
Only that he has far to go
To find a refuge safe and sound
Somewhere deep beneath the ground.

Nature's way is hard and rough,
Got to be both hard and tough,
No longer a life or game and play
He's going to have to hunt for prey

Or no dinner he will get
Nor the smell of hounds forget.

G Bailey

DUSK TILL DAWN

The stillness, the silence, is hard to endure,
Each time as I turn my key in the door,
A hall so empty, no wag of a tail,
No barks of delight to say all is well,
I gaze at the picture that hangs on the wall,
One moment is magic then tears start to fall,
How can one dog cause so much pain,
That nothing else matters, not even the rain,
I move to the kitchen to make some more tea,
I see his eyes everywhere, looking at me,
I remember the day when I brought him home,
How he puddled on every mat I owned,
I touch his lead on the kitchen door,
Memories flood back more and more,
As weeks slip past, tears cease to fall,
But the sighs and emptiness say it all,
Dear Bill I will love you forever more.
Then one dreary night as I wend my way home,
I see a small pup on the path all alone,
I touch the poor little shivering soul,
It cannot be more than a few weeks old,
I pick it up gently and hurry on home,
Into the kitchen, it is warm by the stove,
The pup wags its tail, it seems quite bold,
Everything in the room suddenly glows,
What is happening, it feels like the dawn
And you little pup, my Bill reborn.

Jean Kington

HUNTING

Some days I cannot coax my cat to eat,
No matter how I tempt, or bribe, or treat.
Offerings of poultry, meat or fish
Are greeted with his tail's disdainful swish.

Without a trace of guilt, or mew of pardon
He leaves me, to go hunting in the garden.
A passing slug is easy prey, but rubbery;
A better hunting-ground lay in the shrubbery.

There is no sound from stealthy, padded feet;
A creeping juniper joins in the deceit.
The greyness of his fur, and shadowed zone
Lend him, at rest, resemblance to a stone.

No scrutiny, how careful, gives a sign
That nature hides from nature this feline;
Until, with ears prick'd, the sound of flapping
Rouses my grey hunter from his napping.

Cover is uncovered, stone is stirred
As, watching from his hide, he sees a bird.
Launching himself, and clawing at the air,
He flails grotesquely, like a dancing bear.

Tho' senses strain, and sinews work together,
Nothing is gained, except a broken feather.
Green eyes track his prey, high in a tree
And, snarling at defeat, turns home for tea.

A A Greenleaf

DOG SHOW

The crowd was very still and silent, with tension running high,
Competitors with racing hearts knew the judge's choice was nigh.
The dogs were all oblivious as they languished on their leashes,
With shampooed hair and brushed out tails and names like 'Zak' and 'Peaches'
The lucky dog was called out front for a cup and red rosette,
But all the other owners thought their own dogs better pets.

                 So,
Geraldine stood with her feet firmly planted, her razor cut turned to the sky,
Then strode at a brisk pace, and flung back her shoulders, (I fancied a warrior's cry.)
Her bosom was heaving with pent up emotion, her twin-set was straining across,
She fixed the poor judge with a steely, cold grimace, she must let him know who was boss!
And Cynthia swept Archie into her arms, raised her chin and stalked off in a mood,
Shouting, 'Judge you're as a blind as a bat in dark glasses,' and other things equally rude.
Poor Nigel was crying and wringing his hanky, while Fifi got covered in tears,
'Her psyche will be damaged, her doggie emotions, she'll never recover for years!
When I think of the time that we spent at the salon! With tinting and spraying and trimming',
Not to mention the grooming I did on poor Fifi, and all of those weeks I spent slimming!
The Brigadier bellowed 'This just isn't cricket!' And blew out his handlebar 'tache,
He advanced on the judge with much, 'bahing' and 'umphing', and cries of 'I say, balderdash!'
Now Geraldine smoothed down the hem of her tweed skirt, and swept someone's pup off her brogue

'March forth dogs for honour, we should take the cup home, we all know this judge is a rogue!'
In a forest of dogs' legs and furious people, the judge was pulled down to the ground,
He vowed never again to attempt 'Judge's favourite,' for a million, squillion pounds!

J Christie

GULF WAR HERO

Where's the young kid with the freckles?
Oh! He's been taken home to blighty, God Almighty,
He's only been here for a week.
They say his mother didn't know
just up and joined the marines,
he did it for a dare, or so it seems.
Crazy kid he needs a kicking,
he just got a good licking
lost his legs, so they say, crazy kid.
He'll tell them back at home
stories they won't believe,
But we're trained for land and sea, we'll get 'em wait and see,
We'll see them rot in hell before we leave.
Jesus, here they come again
Someone get us out of this place . . .
Don't turn him over, please don't turn him over
I cannot bear to see another blackened face . . .
He's bought it.

Caren Jayne

ANIMALS, WHO WANTS THEM?

Animals, who wants them? They're always in the way.
Cats and dogs get everywhere, no matter what you say.
You've just cleaned all the house and you sit down on your chair;
You know you will get up and find dirty paw marks everywhere!

You get up early morning to go and see your horse.
You have to rush to get to work but the horse comes first of course.
And when you get home tired from a long and trying day,
You have to go and see him first, make sure he's got some hay.

Tinned food or hay to purchase, the cost seems awful high,
But you just have to pay it, though you do it with a sigh.
Meals always must be served on time. They'll complain if you are late.
If you have not had time to eat, then you just have to wait.

But should you ever lose them, you really are distraught.
Your dearest friend is missing, that is your only thought.
No more the loving nuzzle, soft fur or proffered paw;
It's then you really understand how sweet life was before.

You'd give the world to feed them, though it used to be a chore.
You know if you don't find them nothing matters anymore.
A false alarm, thank goodness, they weren't that long away;
But it can make you realise how they brighten up your day.

Animals, who wants them? They're always in the way.
It really doesn't matter though, we love them anyway.
And all the work, cost, trouble, doesn't matter in the end:
Be it horse, cat, dog or smaller pet, you know you've got a friend.

T Betty Chadwick

A CAT'S 'TAIL'

Two white gloves and two white socks a coat so soft and black.
Strong whiskers from a handsome face, I'm a photogenic cat
I know just how to use my charm to always get my way
A cute expression is the key to let me out to play
When darkness falls I softly tread the way up to a bed
I choose the softest duvet to rest my weary head
Sometimes I wake and feel so bored and seek my catnip mouse
It bounces off my master's head and wakens up the house
He will not remonstrate with me for I know what to do
I sit and look so woebegone and then I start to mew
Some months ago I had no home and wandered all around
But now I am contented with the happiness I've found.

Audrey Robbins

DIRTY WINDOWS

We're gazing out through dirty windows -
Where's the world we used to know?
The trees have turned the strangest colour
There's poison falling with the snow.
What on Earth have we been doing?
Nature's ways are all undone
The sky itself looks down in anger,
At the damage done by man.
The forests are screaming for redemption
As land is claimed by flowing mud -
Now's the time to check the balance
Before the rivers run with blood.

A L Griffin

SHORT BUT TRUE!

We concrete their earth
And pollute the sea
Destroy their spirits
And the air they breathe
Yet joyous love they long to share
With you and me, who really care.

Mary Czornenkyj

THE WAR IS OVER

The war is over
and peace is here,
Hopefully it will stay
For many a year.

No more sirens
ringing aloud,
No more guns
killing the crowd.

No more people
running around,
No more faces
hitting the ground.

The war is over
and peace is here,
Hopefully it will stay
For many a year.

Vicky Burke

THE BANTAM COCK

Rescued he was, the Bantam cock
From strutting busy city streets,
And taken to a rural plock
Where crowings were accepted feats.

He quickly led the little band
Of Warren hens and took their eye
Cavorting round the verdant land
Which overlooks the sylvan Wye.

Each morn he crowed to north and south
The hens looked on and were impressed
At eventide with open mouth
Proclaimed his views to east and west.

Alas one dawn the farmer spied
A missing hen, when door unlocks,
He thought perhaps the hen had died
Out in the field - or was it fox?

A search was made of ground and hedge
No tell-tale feathers to be seen
The buildings probed, each nook and ledge,
No clue revealed where hen had been.

The days went by and then a week
But still no trace of Warren hen
The farmer planned no more to seek
From past experience said 'Amen'.

Three weeks elapsed - the plot now thickens
The cock starts crowing with delight
Home came the hen with thirteen chickens
The cock had proved himself outright.

William Austin Pugh

RETURN TO EXMOOR

How long has it been?
It seems a lifetime
since I was last here.
Since I thrilled to the
wildness of this place,
breathed its loneliness,
and lost myself in the
sounds of morning.

How good it seems
watching a fox angle a
hillside where thistle has
grown, seeing him move
through the mist to the
moorland, and stretching
my mind just to be
where he roams.

To a wideness of purple
and shades of green
where hawk and blackthorn
scorn the wind, and every
timeless combe and rise
hides in its bracken
silver streams.

Shimmering overlays for stones
and mosses where in deeper
pools the water slows to
mirror yet another day,
and soon, maybe, a fox
who drinks, and lingers
on his way.

Graham Biddlecombe

THE HUMAN RACE

As I sit here playing music
And my thoughts begin to drift
A lot of men are too sick
To appreciate the gift
Of life that they've been given
Each moment of the time
Allowed to them for living
Or to contemplate a crime

What right has man that he denies
The basic needs of life
To countless species, so their cries
Cut through you like a knife.
The forest's gone, the seasons fail
The skies are black with smoke
And this is on a world-wide scale
It isn't just a joke.

We blunder, plunder, use, abuse
Take what we want, and kill
Whatever else gets in our way
We'll carry on until
There's nothing left; it makes me so
Ashamed to be a part
The human race must all be blamed
It hasn't got a heart.

If only we could start again,
Line up and take our place
Begin again, the main event
The final, human race.

Ros Nancarrow

THESE HUMANS

O the beauty of our mother earth
Blue waters and golden sands
Sunny skies all flowering birth
Running rivers through wooded lands
Mighty mountains cap in white
All this beauty within our sight
Pastures green and granite hills
Snowy slopes with all these thrills.

All went wrong with the birth of man
Till the land and kill its game
Axe the trees - his want of land
Dam the rivers - within his name
Caged the animals - such horrible zoos
So in the end - who owns who
Put his mark on all he kills
All he says he's not ill.

Makes the law to suit his own
Rides around in old tin cans
Pollutes the air for all he can
Sells the food and what is sown
Feeds his children ecstasy pills
Putting right their inner ills
If not him - who has the will.

Man says dogs - must not crap
Garden greens and pavement mats
Tho' he craps - all into the seas
Fish swimming through in his breeze
Do animals condemn - men and mates
Crawling humans - out of the bog.

E T Ward

NUMBERING TUMBLING LAPWING

If you're lucky, one day
in early spring you might see
a bright posturing male lapwing,
tumbling about in swooping display
above a grassy green pasture.

From undulating ground
he swiftly rises, rolling and falling
as though he's senseless, and is quite losing all flight control,
flaps his dark wings in noisy rasping beats,
utters a few ecstatic, rhythmic wheezy bubbling notes.
His underside and bright
cheek patches flash white
against a contrasted black, sharply pointed face.
His long upswept crest quivers,
broad bulging wings shimmer
in blue - purple iridescent sheen.

Sad to say, in a great many
open country parts of Britain today,
springtime lapwing tumbling is fast becoming a fading memory;
we're losing our burbling flapwing clapwing,
the number of birds is dwindling, has been declining
for forty years or more, is probably around two-thirds what it was,
as spring nesting on ploughed ground is made tricky
by cultivating crops that are too tall and dense,
and livestock far too many for common-sense
around pastures near their nests, best suited to rearing chicks,
so they have altogether gone from large farmland areas.

Our native bird is now being replaced
by winter visitor flocks flickering over from the continent,
although as agriculture everywhere ever relentlessly intensifies,
their lapwing numbers also are tumbling.

David Daymond

THE DYING BEAST

He lies there just dying
Breathing in his last air
Remembering the good times
When he could go anywhere.

His breathing is so heavy
As the blood is flowing out
The bullet in his side
He wished it was out

The pain is getting stronger
As he tries not to move
There's voices all around him
And he is shoved and is pulled

With his black silky coat
He could hide in the dark
But dogs and their men friends
Just shot at his heart

No more will he run free
No more will he hunt
He lies dead before them
As they start to cut him up

They killed him for pleasure
And killed him for fun
Destroyed all the good things
Which God has built strong.

Susan Davies

THE BUCK STOPS HERE

Rabbit is as rabbit does,
In and out the hole, he was
Always in a hurry, always in a spin,
Out of warren, round the field and in
Again. With all his playmates,
Over ditch and under gate.
Fleet of foot and long of ear.
Dances, dusk and dawn, no fear
Encroaches on his fun,
Except for fox, and man and gun.

Deborah Aston

THE CHRISTMAS MEANING

What is there left to say about
our Christmas day.
The holly and the ivy all picked
to deck the halls
The Christmas tree in the corner
with twinkling lights and coloured
balls.

But wait, it's not just these things
that give a festive ring,
It is more to do with the journey,
made by those three kings.

The shepherds also made the trek
coming from afar.
And, at the end lay Jesus, and
overhead the star.

Margarita Reeve

WELCOME ABOARD

Captain Noah wishes you a pleasant cruise aboard the Ark!
We shall be cruising at a height of zero feet above sea level.
The forecast is a little stormy, with further heavy rain.

Noah wasn't stupid, he wasn't inept -
But have you ever wondered where they all slept?

He would need:

A collection of kennels to house cats and dogs
And hutches for cavies and rabbits;
And ponds as a home for the toads and the frogs
And others of freshwater habit.

How did he manage the lairs for the bears,
And where were the dens for the foxes?
And how did he cater for open-air hares?
Or did everything have to use boxes?

The birds could make nests at the top of a pole
Or perch up aloft on the rigging;
But what about moles, who are happiest in holes?
There'd be nowhere that they could go digging.

Did tucking them up take him ages each night
And did he read long bedtime stories?
By the time that he'd settled them all, was it light?
Did the birds sing a cheerful dawn chorus?

And when, after forty days, all marched ashore -
Or waddled, or galloped or pattered,
Saying farewell with bark, squeak or roar,
Did Noah feel utterly shattered?

Margaret Porter

NATURE'S CABARET

The night was dark as the day came to an end
The winds they sang through a mountain glen
The moon peeps out from the darkened sky
Illuminating clouds that slowly drifted by
In the open fields the hooting birds hover
Field mice squeak and scamper to the hedgerow's cover
When swifts and swallows vanish with the night-time mask
Bats take over feeding off midge as their nocturnal task
Moths replace butterflies fluttering around a camper's fire
Cattle sing their lullabies inside a farmer's byre
Tunes of the nightingale fade as the night becomes undone
The enchanting songbirds' chorale greets the rising sun

Michael Monaghan

THE PHOTOGRAPH

Who are you, person in a photograph?
Snapped out of time into silent space.
Unkind immortality
          no different from the lines the cave men drew.
Or are you more?
In the midst of those who treasure
and adore, no doubt.
Pour over every crinkle, frown or dimple
'Oh! Isn't he lovely. Just like his pa!'

Frame it, enlarge it,
Encased in a locket
Gold, warmed against a beating heart
Would that give you life?

Who are you?

Janet Barbara Berry

THE BAT

Whilst on holiday in Spain
Having drinks at the bar,
Chattering with tourists
And drinking Sangria

They spoke of a bat,
Hung on their balcony sill,
Not welcome up a corner, and
Was hanging there still.

I offered my services,
Unaware of my plight,
Armed with new gardening gloves,
Climbed stairs up, five flights.

The bat hid up a corner,
I caught him with ease,
Held him over the balcony rail
And shook gently to release.

That terrible moment,
Like a bat out of hell,
He released his grip
Down to the concrete he fell.

A conscience of guilt
As we looked over the rail,
Predatory cat ran out,
Ate the bat and turned tail.

A mission of mercy,
We all tried our best -
For a bat with no future
Is now laid to rest.

V Braker

116

FERN

First a shoot;
Then a sprout;
A ball of leaves
Half way out.

Now you grow;
Now you spread.
Where once we walked
You stand instead.

Up you climb,
Tall and strong,
Obscure our views
All summer long.

Hide the flowers;
Hide the game;
Everything green -
Everything the same.

But you hide all the litter
And paper from chips.
And you hide all the lovers
Gyrating their hips.

And you hide our dereliction -
Conceal it from view.
As we use the forest
The forest needs you.

Ian Hodgkinson

THE THIRD SEASON

Russet red, mellow yellow, ochre brown,
crisp and dry they tumble down
to join in a gay tarantella in the breeze;
                    the autumn leaves.

Across the countryside colours blend
from foreground to horizon's end,
vermilion, amethyst, burnt sienna, green;
                    the autumn scene.

High winds put leaves in aviation
trees are bare, a new situation -
Autumn ceases with winds of sorrow;
                    it's winter tomorrow.

Rita Trodd

EPIDEMIC IN THE DARK

I learned of a fatal attraction today,
'I don't care - you've got the death sentence anyway.'
Either straight, homosexual, it doesn't matter,
Epidemic in the dark, served on a platter.
Swept under the carpet, conspiracy ripe.
This diagnosis still appears just a hype.
Vulnerable victims suffer unaware,
That the lover they trust has a virus to share.
Shot in the blood stream, by lethal weapon.
Loss of respect from emotions of passion.
Malicious sufferers pass on the disease,
Hoping that sharing will make the pain ease.
Who is to say that it's wrong to have sex?
With someone agreeing. Who'll soon become ex.
Finding out of the sores, the suffering, the crime.
Funeral bell tolls that endlessly chime.

Louise Salter

PEACE

What is peace? I ask myself
What does it really mean?
Rest in peace
Is carved on tombstones
Grant us peace
Is asked in our prayer
But does anyone know
What it means?
And does anyone really care?

Peace is not, I can say for sure
The expectant quiet
Or tense humidity
Before a raging storm

Peace is tranquillity
A time when you can relax
And let the comfortable drowsiness
Make you sit down and lay back

Peace is the rolling, green hills
The seas of yellow corn
The swaying branches of many trees
The zephyr of dawn

Peace could be expressed
As the time between wars
When governments agree
When races get along
When the armies have a quiet life
And all the tension is gone

Hannah Dutton (14)

A SOLDIER'S THOUGHTS

Bright, light sun,
Cool breathing air,
Clear, with space unbounded.
Hadrian's hills hold Roman secrets.
Aye, and those of conscripts too,
Who laboured at the wall, coast to coast
Sketching a safe place
From the wild marauding mad-men.
Their skill stands still and strong
A proud reminder of our heritage.

How Flavius longs for home.
Stands chilled at the mile castle
Gazing at the grey distant menace
But seeing only a sun-drenched land
Poplars, olive groves, vineyards,
Baking hot courtyards and fountains cool.
He feels not the shivering breezes,
Only the warmth on his back.
He cannot smell the midden,
But the fragrant herb-filled kitchen
Where his plump mother sings all day,
And the perfume of Octavia's skin
Merging with joy in her brown, earthy hair,
Her green eyes wickedly encouraging,
So near, yet out of reach forever.

How much longer in the heather land?
Still tomorrow, a few days' rest
Sheltered a little from the stiff north-easterlies,
Where the musicians are not too bad,
Considering this is England.

Jennifer McNish

REMEMBRANCE 1914-1918

Remember your poppy for Remembrance Day,
Revere our courageous dead,
With rifle in hand and shield of the Lord,
They bravely surged ahead,

They fought them in the trenches,
On land, sea and sky,
Saddened must have been their hearts,
As they watched their comrades die,

As bullets flew around them,
Cannons above them roared,
Many a weary cry was heard,
As they prayed unto the Lord,

As they lay suffering on the ground,
The dying and the maimed,
Oh! When will mankind ever learn,
That nothing from war is gained,

They fought for King and country,
For the likes of you and me,
Thousands fought and died for us,
That we may all be free,

So whenever you see a poppy,
That flower of flaming red,
Just ponder a while and remember,
Those brave and courageous dead.

Irene Latheron

VE DAY 1945

People laughing,
singing, dancing,
linking arms
and holding hands.
People hugging,
cuddling, kissing,
moving slowly
down the Strand.
People splashing
in the fountains,
climbing high
on every tree;
youngsters swinging
from the lampposts
waving colours
excitedly.
Throngs of people
crowd the railings
calling for the
King and Queen,
they appear midst
cheers and clapping,
smiling, waving
graciously.
The war is over,
great rejoicing!
For the heroes -
a welcoming.

But sitting quietly,
weeping, mourning,
those whose loved ones
did not return.

Joan Miles Lister

A PLEA TO RWANDA

In Rwanda today, peace seems far, far away.
War and conflict touch all and there's hate.
Was it always the same before its new name,
When the white man was there to dictate?

Did foreign dominion used to focus opinion,
Where suspicion and hate could be aimed?
And when they pulled out, was there no-one about
To take their complaints or be blamed?

What now is perceived with independence achieved?
Do their peoples together progress?
No, the tribes are all fighting instead of uniting
And we now have division and stress.

Why now be derisive instead of decisive?
Your new country with promise is full
And by standing as one in whatever needs done
You'll succeed when together you pull.

Why fan tribal fears and go on fighting for years,
When in forests and mountains so vast
There's enough for each man, whatever his clan,
Be it Hutu or Tutsi his caste?

As incentive for all, you may like to recall
The days you were ruled by state minions,
And the white man's beliefs, with scant heed to your chiefs,
Were implemented despite their opinions.

Let your arguments cease and your tribes live in peace.
To this goal as one you must strive,
So abolish your hate and improve on your fate,
For in friendship you'll prosper and thrive.

John McLean

WAR

Far from home
Across the sea,
In a trackless land
There's a grave for me.
Where camels thirst
And vultures reign,
In the desert heat
I fell, slain.
No willows weep
Above my stone,
Just shifting sand
Eroding bone.
For King and country
And all that's right,
To war I went,
A foe to fight.
For the same ideals
My father's blood,
On a Flanders field,
Ebbed in the mud.
In compensation
For our loss,
Our names are engraved
On a cold stone cross'
It stands alone
In a market square,
Recalling men
Whose fate, we share.

Whole generations
Lost in sorrow,
To bequeath to you
A good tomorrow,
Why did we die,
Was it all in vain.
For in Sarajevo
There's war again.

John Bracken

MUSIC IS LOVE

Music is moods
Music is love
Music descends from heaven above.

Music is quiet
Music is sweet
Music's for dancing your way down the street.

Music is soft
Music is slow
Music will follow where e'er lovers go.

Music can sing
Music can cry
Music can soar like a lark in the sky.

Music is magic
Music has powers
Music's for lovers - therefore it's ours.

Anne Clegg

BY CHOICE

Mother earth revolts, a final winter, black and bitter cold
The jackals cohort, death, satanic evil, corrupting all men
Chattering gatlings and government lies, their message told
Allied thus, reaping harvest with bullet and devious pen

Feuding dictators wield as vast weapons of strife
Food and water, withheld, until lands are conceded
Repressed nations in bondage, despair for their lives
Generals conspire, whilst humanity lies, unheard, unheeded

People pray to their Gods, beg for redemption
Earth takes her revenge, for destruction and waste
The reaper gathers all, hell makes no exceptions
Angels of death growl, for blood's hot, fetid taste

Come then you warriors, armed and girded for battle
Snarling, heathen eyes, red blooded with rage
Pagans lusting for carnage, slaughter like cattle
Earth shudders, cries out, as they write the last page

World ramparts lie smashed, countries ravished, rent asunder
Immortal prophets cry for fields, red sodden, deathly still
Tyrants' armies thrashed, cower, stare up in wonder
As the chosen ones' followers swarm down from the hills

Stillness shrouds the terrestrial stage, dark, empty without a star
Mankind's greed engulfs all, in world-wide degradation
Angels gather souls, lost, victims of the final holy war
The players banished, no knights left to fight for man's salvation

T Bates

WHAT A LOVELY SIGHT TO SEE

What a lovely sight to see,
Snowflakes drifting down through the trees.
Their branches are bare, except for a bird or two,
And where the snowflakes land.

The mountains so high,
Where the fir trees stand,
With their branches spread out,
They nearly touch the ground.
And as the snowflakes fall, down to the ground,
There is snow lying all around,
It is a proper winter wonderland.

Margaret Coleman

POOR TEDDY BEAR

Teddy Bear, Teddy Bear
Took a spill
Yes, Teddy Bear, Teddy Bear
Felt terribly ill.
So he sent for the doctor
Said doctor come quick,
I really am feeling
Awfully sick.

So the doctor he came
And he felt Teddy's head.
Yes you have a big bump
Now go straight to bed.
Have a good rest
And take these pills,
I promise that that
Will cure all your ills.

So Teddy he did
What the doctor had said,
He took his pills
And he stayed in bed.
In a few days
He felt just like new.
Now Teddy would like
To come play with you.

Valerie Lloyd

THE LAST GOODBYE

With ageing limbs we stand
  On the headstoned green surround.
Focused thoughts fixed reverently
  On the lush but foreign land.
This goodbye is now the last,
  A finality, on this hallowed ground.

Fifty years and more they've lain,
  In perfect peace, un-aged,
The years at last have taken toll
  If us beside the rustic gallic lane.
The breeze that stirs the ancient dust,
  Whips up, as limp, still flags are disarranged.

Unashamedly the tears descend,
  To fuse with soil that now, forever,
Encapsulates our memories,
  To stay with us to journey's end.
The ending soon for us will beckon,
  As we bid a last goodbye, and links to sever.

A mile across the waving wheat,
  Other stones cast shadows against the sunlit sky.
For just a generation had passed,
  Then these men's fathers fell where we now sadly meet,
Would that they could hear our silent prayer,
  And a question for God, oh why, oh why, oh why?

Iolo Lewis

FROM WHERE I STAND

All right, I'm old.
Have I been here too long
To be inspired by bold
Young people, full of song
For mother Earth, this planet?

128

Nature cares for youth
But when you're old how can it
Care? Just face the truth:
The aged feel the cold,
They dread a sneeze,
And few but the very old
Know all about disease.

Still, through it all a joy
To lift my load -
That smile of girl and boy
New-started on life's road.

V H Anderson

THE FUTURE

Just read the Bible, and you will see,
What the future holds eventually,
Famines and earthquakes in diverse places,
Discord and hatred in many races.
Children defying fathers and mothers,
Sisters often betraying their brothers.
A horrible thing in the temple will stand,
If you see it, fly from the land.
There will be terror, so fierce to behold,
The sun will not shine, the moon will grow cold,
Many stars from Heaven will fall,
There will be trouble for one and all.
Then from the clouds the Lord will appear
All will see Him in trembling and fear.
He will descend in great glory and power,
'Watch' said Jesus 'You know not that hour.'

Eugenie Barker

TRIBULATION

The die is cast, the stage is set,
The day of truth has dawned, not yet,
With no respite the tyrant's might
Brings fear by day and death by night
To the high hills they all have fled
But find no solace there, instead,
They face cold snow to chill their limbs
And misery, starvation brings.
Their cries of anguish float on high
And go, unanswered to God's sky
But still the tyrant follows on
Intent to kill them, every one.
If they proceed, that poor sad race,
The door is shut in every face
And backwards now they fear to go
For death is waiting in the snow.
Because they would not bow the knee
To the devil who ruled their own country.

My eyes have seen, my heart has known,
This misery that could be my own.
The fate we all may have to bear
While the devil rules God's earth so fair.
It seems that God can't bear to see
The injustice of their misery.
The strong, the weak, the sick and blind
Have fled to leave Iraq behind.
The starving children, cold as ice,
Seem like a human sacrifice,
To pacify the tyrant king,
And all the trials his power doth bring.
He does not sleep, the God on high,
He hears the prayers rise in his sky
And knows that vengeance for this sin
When the time is right, belongs to him.

Pamela Harris

NATURE STRIKES BACK

The ocean roars back
It can't hold back
I'm frozen by the power
Of cold grey on black

Pleading for mercy
Trapped by the sound
I'm afraid of dying
When no trace is found

Lost in the desert
A sun burns red
And distant horizons
Stay far ahead

This moving oasis
This trick of the brain
And when I touch it
I'm only insane

The forest is lord
I'm at its command
Completely surrounded
By this masterplan

Trees sway in secret
Stealing the sun
As I scream in darkness
My time has come

Nature strikes back
Stealing the mind
And what comes to take me
Is cruel and kind

Nature stikes back
It's got to attack . . .

Bernard Harry Reay

131

PEACE TALKS?

The tragic story of wars
Is hardly one for applause
Bloody action out of doors
Intrigue behind closed doors

The horrors of the conflict
So keen are they to depict
But never on your life
The full reasons for the strife

Talks start early these days
Its part of our modern ways
World opinion is a good tool
But who are they trying to fool

Peace discussed at the table
Each does what he is able
Not so much to stop the war
But for his side get much more

In the talking from the start
Vanity plays its part
The loss of face inside
Tops loss of life outside

Talking alone just won't do
Hostile backup's needed too

If as seems to be the course
Force only yields to force
Keep it small as can be
Forget your military

The victims must be few
And be the right ones too
So when they have the talks
Employ a new Guy Fawkes.

Harry Derx

THE DESTRUCTION OF THE EARTH

Once fowls were free, the speckled hen a gladsome
sight, searched in the yard and orchard green, a
roosting shed by night,
'pon what she found with scraps and corn, enjoy
a new day dawn.
Fine feather trim, red comb, bright eye, with feet held high,
she strutted by.
Her handsome cockerel crowed, they ate the herbitage they chose
Eggs layed, in nest box bed, a thoughtfully, constructed shed.
Strong shells to prove the cockerel spoke, rich
orange, golden yolk.
She gave, became a slave to man, whom in his
greed takes every egg he can.
Confined to darkness, cramped in tiny cage,
perpetual 'lectric light engage.
Deprived of air and sky, her eggs pulled from her,
soon she die.
None go to waste, end up a fancy biscuits, slabs of cake.
All male chicks die, no good for meat be found,
Millions a day, gassed, suffocated, drowned,
Man, the vilest predator of all, his own kind kills unborn.
Will take until the Earth's heart break, twist
nature's course, pollute and force.
Beware Black Spring will come, no leaf, or blossom, sun.
Earth bare, desolate, a tomb, soon mirror, sister moon.
And men as blind as worms, will grovel in the gloom.

A E Doney

ENCHANTMENT

Translucent nights in early June
Gentle breezes bring a tune
Music made by dragonfly wings
Or maybe fairies as they sing
Visions of light in mosses green
Cobwebs of silk, for a fairy queen

It is a dream within a dream
When fairies dance
By the running stream
Grasses of shimmering velvet
Beneath their tiny feet
Sparkling in the moonlight
With early morning dew
Under the spell
Of the fairy dell
Where dreams can come true

R F Kelly

TREES ACROSS THE PARK

Oh but they are beautiful,
The trees across the park
Their branches twined like arteries
Around the living heart.
A million years of time and space
They stood and dreamed and grew
So Man could live and breathe, and fight
And hide in them, and eat the fruit
And light his fires at night.

Oh but they are dead and gone
The trees across the park.
Last night men came with grinding saws
And bit into the bark.
Once stretching wide from coast to coast
They stood in serried rank
While Man was crawling from the ooze
And what is left? - A plank.

Dory Phillips

SCREEN WITH TEARS

Time's illusion in a lace
Turns once more to wonder's face
Touched again by memory's hinge
Streisand's vocal heartfelt strings

While away from silent times
And an era's happy mime
Cherish now nostalgia's sting
Jerking tears of Redford-ing

Simple moments crassly had
As a playground's huffy lad
Would have shared a secret's note
If a boy had talked one load

Home's a place confirmed again
Stuck inside an outer hem
Wishing more to icy lads
Barbara's song melts shyer fads

David Bennett

FOR LOUISE

She's gone to heaven that lovely young girl
She's gone to heaven and her family is in hell
She went missing early on Christmas morning
She'd been out dancing in her best frock
She wasn't wearing it when they found her
They found her two months later in the quarry
Two young boys who'd gone looking for adventure
Saw her decomposing on a ledge

She's gone to heaven she'll never grow old
She's gone to heaven because he murdered her
His evil hands forced her spirit from her body
May his eyes remember her face
And the last close of her eyes
May he be haunted by her cries
May he remember the feel of her skin
And the texture of her long hair
May his conscience violate him
Forever

Julia Wallis-Bradford

SPRING JINGLE

I saw green buds on the lilac tree
Though now it was only February.
Still, Marcle Hills were lined with snow
But till the echoing white blossoms blow
High on Dog Hill, where the wild cherries grow
Spring won't have come to Ledbury.

Rosemary Farrow

THE DANCING RIVER

The river is dancing, through the valley below,
Flowing past ground, where wild daisies grow.
Past protruding rocks, which have been there, for years,
On, to a place, where it splits, with no fears.

Splits into two, then joins back, into one,
Travelling so swiftly, like it's having such fun.
On past the rapids, as it heads for the sea,
Gathering speed, when the tide's out, you see.

For the river is tidal, and when the tide's in,
It slows down the pace, of the river's travelling.
It joins the sea, eventually, come what may,
A perfect fusion, here to stay.

River meets sea, and the fish know the smell,
Of the river, they came from, they always can tell.
They wait for the rain, to replenish the rivers,
Then when it arrives, they never do dither.

They're ready to travel, the river from whence they came,
A life-form, now visiting, to give life once again.
The call of nature, to fish in the sea,
The rains come, to make their destiny.

Now easier to travel, and negotiate, as they reach for
Their spawning ground, never too late.
To carry out their duties, now in the river,
I watch now the eels, as slowly they slither.

Their food source, now changed, to freshwater food once again,
They were totally relying, on that downpour of rain.
They're finding it easier, much easier to travel,
To a new home, with a bed, a bed made from gravel.

Stephen T Maslen

THE ENGLISH LOVE THEIR TEA

Where e'er I go, 'cross land and sea, it does occur to me,
The people there, as I'm aware, reject the taste of tea,
Coffee is their current brew, in America that's fine,
In France and Spain, and Italy, the normal brew is wine.
I don't know how they know these things, it's quite a mystery,
Remote as many places are, they offer us our tea.

The tea plant grows, as all who knows, in India, Assam,
In Ceylon too, the tea plants grew, by economic plan.
China tea is green you see, a product of fermenting,
They drink it from such tiny cups, and sup it unrelenting.
Our clipper ships would bring it here, from Shanghai and Bombay,
It made a lot of money for the wealthy, and it stayed.

Cutty Sark, a clipper ship, preserved at Greenwich Dock,
Was just the craft, from fore to aft, that carried this fine stock.
So it is said, am I misled, a war was really fought,
Over English tea in the colony, the area, New York.
A tax was raised, and caused outrage, at the port of Boston,
The British settlers out there, would drink their tea quite often.

Three clippers from East India, docked after months at sea,
They were attacked, their cargoes dumped, into the flooded quay.
The *Boston Tea Party*, as was known, in seventeen seventy three,
The tax imposed was never paid, by a colonist decree.
The years that followed led to the war, of independency,
Which finally succeeded, in seventeen eighty three.

The army brew, and this is true, is sweet and thick, you see,
And they all stop at three o'clock, to have a mug of tea.
So long ago, I guess it's so, that Wellington agrees,
To stop the fight at Waterloo, in time to have their teas.
So well may we remember that, the English love their tea,
And woe betide a stranger, who denies their liberty.

D Firsht

MR RHEESE'S QUAINT SWEET SHOP

Two little cottages side by side
Of the one do dwell Mr and Mrs Rheese.
The front room is a sweet shop so quaint inside,
Large jars of sweets and sherbet on display.
Sweets and chocs of many choice - sherbet make pop for today.

Mr Rheese a large stout, stern man,
Sit outside stop on wooden chair, whenever he can.
Silver watch and chain hang proudly across waist-coat,
On head wear a Dai Cap, a proud man - not one to boast.
He light up his old clay pipe, watch passers by with comfort delight.

Once a year all children given a treat . . .
A free liquorice pipe and whirl, a bag of sweets.
As children line up outside the shop in single file
Old Rheese stamp each left hand, held out eagerly for a while.
No earthly chance of cheating and coming back, children smile.

His little quiet wife with neat hair of grey,
Serve the children with gifts this day, and wait for the thank you say.
Always lived with the old believe . . .
Children never to be heard, but so often to be seen.
Happy are the girls' smile, and the boys' wide grin,
As the black liquorice dribbled from mouth down the chin.
Wipe off with old jersey sleeve of navy blue
Wave to old Rheese, make way to park, have a swing or two.

'Swing low, swing high, nearly reach Heaven sky
O'er the stark and dark Cwm pit, feet seems to go
See the coloured rainbow o'er Cwm pit softly glow
In the land of Our Fathers for evermore.

Phyllis Blue

A TALE

Have you heard the tale,
Of a mop and pale,
That went cleaning,
One bright sunny morning,
Said, the pale to the mop.
I cannot hop,
With all this water inside me,
Empty it out and give me chance
To show you, just what I can do,
The mop did that,
And the little brat,
Began to do a dance.

Elsie Keen

INFORMATION

We hope you have enjoyed reading this book - and that you will continue to enjoy it in the coming years.

If you like reading and writing poetry drop us a line, or give us a call, and we'll send you a free information pack.

Write to

Arrival Press Information
1-2 Wainman Road
Woodston
Peterborough
PE2 7BU